Passive Income

Easy Ways to Start an Online Business, Create a Passive Income Stream

(How Affluent Investors Build Generational Wealth)

Andrew Davis

Published By **Oliver Leish**

Andrew Davis

All Rights Reserved

Passive Income: Easy Ways to Start an Online Business, Create a Passive Income Stream (How Affluent Investors Build Generational Wealth)

ISBN 978-1-7774626-8-0

No part of this guidebook shall be reproduced in any form without permission in writing from the publisher except in the case of brief quotations embodied in critical articles or reviews.

Legal & Disclaimer

The information contained in this book is not designed to replace or take the place of any form of medicine or professional medical advice. The information in this book has been provided for educational & entertainment purposes only.

The information contained in this book has been compiled from sources deemed reliable, and it is accurate to the best of the Author's knowledge; however, the Author cannot guarantee its accuracy and validity and cannot be held liable for any errors or omissions. Changes are periodically made to this book. You must consult your doctor or get professional medical advice before using any of the suggested remedies, techniques, or information in this book.

Upon using the information contained in this book, you agree to hold harmless the Author from and against any damages, costs, and expenses, including any legal fees potentially resulting from the application of any of the information provided by this guide. This disclaimer applies to any damages or injury caused by the use and application, whether directly or indirectly, of any advice or information presented, whether for breach of contract, tort, negligence, personal injury, criminal intent, or under any other cause of action.

You agree to accept all risks of using the information presented inside this book. You need to consult a professional medical practitioner in order to ensure you are both able and healthy enough to participate in this program.

Table Of Contents

Chapter 1: Understanding Passive Income 1

Chapter 2: Building A Strong Financial Foundation 19

Chapter 3: Investing For Passive Income 36

Chapter 4: Real Estate Investing 52

Chapter 5: Stock Market Investing 67

Chapter 6: Dividend Investing 83

Chapter 7: Creating Passive Income Through Entrepreneurship................... 100

Chapter 8: Maximizing Passive Income Through Side Hustles 117

Chapter 9: Achieving Financial Freedom 131

Chapter 10: Living Your Best Life.......... 144

Chapter 11: Types Of Passive Income .. 155

Chapter 1: Understanding Passive Income

Passive profits is a concept that has won some of hobby in present day years, and for correctly motive. It's a way of incomes earnings that allows you to generate earnings without actively strolling for it. This way that you may earn coins at the same time as you sleep, journey, or experience your free time. In this chapter, we are able to discover the concept of passive earnings in greater element and speak why it is an critical part of carrying out monetary freedom.

Passive earnings can come from an entire lot of belongings, which incorporates condo homes, investments, and virtual products. The key characteristic of passive income is that it calls for very little ongoing try to keep. This is in assessment to lively profits, which requires ongoing artwork to generate income. For example, if you artwork a 9-to-five task, your income is lively earnings. You're replacing your time and effort for money. In contrast, passive profits is generated with out the want for ongoing artwork or attempt.

One of the biggest advantages of passive income is the liberty it offers. When you've got got got a passive profits movement, you've got have been given greater control over it slow and may attention at the topics that do not forget maximum to you. For example, if you have a apartment property that generates passive income, you can spend some time journeying, spending time with own family, or pursuing pursuits and pastimes. This freedom is a key part of reaching economic freedom and dwelling existence in your private phrases.

Passive income additionally offers a sense of protection. When you rely genuinely on lively income, you are at risk of project loss, economic downturns, and unique sudden sports. With passive income, you have got were given a couple of streams of profits that could provide a safety internet inside the path of hard times. This delivered safety can reduce strain and provide more peace of mind.

One of the most famous sorts of passive income is apartment assets. Rental homes can offer a steady circulate of profits and can apprehend in charge over time. For example, in case you buy a rental property for $ hundred,000 and hire it out for $1,500 constant with month, you could generate a month-to-month cash flow of $500 or extra after costs. Over time, due to the fact the belongings appreciates in charge, you may sell it for a earnings and generate even more profits.

Investing is each other popular manner to generate passive income. Investing in shares, bonds, and distinctive financial devices can provide a regular glide of earnings with out the want for ongoing work or strive. For example, in case you spend money on dividend-paying stocks, you could earn a ordinary go with the flow of earnings from the dividends. Over time, due to the fact the value of the shares increases, you could sell them for a profit and generate even greater profits.

Digital products are a few different manner to generate passive income. This includes such things as eBooks, online courses, and digital downloads. Once you create the product, you can sell it over and over with out the want for ongoing artwork or attempt. For example, in case you create an eBook on a popular difficulty matter variety and promote it online, you could generate a drift of earnings for future years.

In this financial disaster, we've got were given explored the idea of passive earnings and mentioned why it is an important part of achieving monetary freedom. We've checked out a number of the wonderful techniques to generate passive income, in conjunction with condominium houses, investments, and virtual merchandise. With passive profits, you can accumulate more monetary and private safety, and live life to your personal terms.

1.1 The advantages of passive earnings

Passive income refers to a go with the go with the flow of income that generates profits with out you actively appealing inside the normal sports activities activities that generate the income. In one of a type words, it's far a manner of earning income on the identical time as you sleep, devour or take a holiday. Passive profits gives monetary freedom and independence, that might bring about a higher fantastic of life. The advantages of passive profits are numerous, and they encompass the subsequent:

Firstly, passive income offers a supply of monetary balance. With passive income, you've got were given a constant motion of income that you may depend on, which can help you sense extra regular to your monetary destiny. Passive earnings can provide a experience of safety in the face of lifestyles's surprising activities, which encompass interest loss, monetary downturns, or medical emergencies. For instance, when you have invested in dividend-paying shares, you may attain regular income from the dividends, even though the stock rate drops.

Secondly, passive profits offers extra time freedom. With passive profits, you have were given more time to pursue your passions, hobbies, or interests. You can spend time together along with your own family, tour, or paintings on a non-public project without having to worry approximately a traditional 9-to-5 method. Passive income offers the opportunity to stay lifestyles in your very very own terms and may help lessen stress and beautify traditional properly-being.

Thirdly, passive income will let you gain financial goals quicker. With the more earnings flow into from passive income, you can hold more money or invest more to your portfolio, which assist you to acquire your financial desires faster. For instance, in case your intention is to retire early, you could spend money on apartment houses that generate passive income and use the apartment profits to store extra money toward your retirement.

Fourthly, passive earnings gives a supply of income that calls for plenty less strive. With passive profits, you do no longer need to actively artwork for every dollar you earn. This approach that you can have more loose time to pursue wonderful interests, spend time on the side of your family, or lighten up. Passive profits also can offer a deliver of earnings that is not relying in your bodily abilties or health.

Fifthly, passive income affords the opportunity to construct wealth over the years. With the compounding impact of passive earnings, you can construct wealth over the years while not having to actively artwork for it. For example, if you put money into dividend-paying shares, the dividends can be reinvested to shop for greater stocks, that might lead to even better dividends inside the future. Over time, this can bring about big wealth accumulation.

Sixthly, passive earnings gives the possibility to create a legacy. With passive earnings, you may leave a legacy for destiny generations. For instance, you could invest in apartment homes and pass them on on your kids as a supply of income. This can help your children advantage financial freedom and independence, and create an prolonged-lasting legacy on your circle of relatives.

In quit, passive income gives severa benefits that can bring about a better outstanding of life. It offers monetary balance, time freedom, the possibility to reap monetary dreams quicker, requires much less effort, the possibility to assemble wealth over time, and the opportunity to create a legacy. Whether you're trying to retire early, spend extra time collectively at the side of your own family, or pursue your passions, passive earnings will let you accumulate your goals and live existence to your personal phrases.

Passive Income Stream	Benefits
Rental Properties	Earn condo profits with out actively managing the assets
Dividend Stocks	Earn dividends and capital gains with out actively dealing with the investments
Online Business	Work from everywhere with an internet connection and set your very own hours
Royalties from Intellectual Property	Earn royalties on revolutionary works with out actively selling them
Peer-to-Peer Lending	Earn hobby on loans with out actively handling the lending manner

As you could see, there are various fantastic sorts of passive earnings streams that individuals can pursue. By figuring out their goals and interests, humans can create a customized portfolio of passive profits streams with a view to offer them with the economic freedom and protection they desire.

1.2 Types of passive income

Passive earnings can are available various bureaucracy and may be generated from particular assets. Understanding the specific types of passive profits will can help you understand which streams of profits may be suitable for you. In this bankruptcy, we can speak the unique kinds of passive income and offer practical examples of each.

Firstly, rental earnings is a common shape of passive profits. Rental profits is generated from renting out property, which include a residence or apartment. This can offer a regular glide of earnings, mainly if the property is located in a suited location with immoderate call for. For example, if you personal a apartment property in a well-known tourist excursion spot, you may lease it out on structures like Airbnb and generate passive earnings from the rental profits.

Secondly, dividend earnings is another form of passive income. Dividend profits is generated from proudly owning stocks that pay out normal dividends. This can provide a regular motion of profits, especially in case you spend money on businesses with a protracted history of paying out dividends. For example, in case you non-public stocks in a enterprise like Coca-Cola, which has an prolonged statistics of paying out dividends, you may earn passive income from the regular dividend bills.

Thirdly, hobby earnings is a kind of passive profits generated from investments like bonds, certificate of deposit (CDs), and financial monetary savings debts. Interest profits can provide a steady go together with the flow of income, especially if you invest in immoderate-yield bills or bonds. For instance, in case you spend money on a excessive-yield financial financial savings account, you can earn passive income from the hobby earned to your financial savings.

Fourthly, royalty earnings is a form of passive profits generated from progressive works which incorporates books, music, or patents. For instance, if you are an writer and placed up a ebook, you could earn passive earnings from the royalties earned from the earnings of the ebook.

Fifthly, capital profits profits is generated from the sale of belongings like shares, real property, or artwork. This can provide a one-time or occasional flow of profits, particularly in case you put money into belongings that appreciate in fee through the years. For instance, in case you put money into real estate and promote a property for a earnings, you could earn passive income from the capital gains earned from the sale.

Sixthly, accomplice advertising earnings is generated from selling products or services and earning a fee from the sales made through your referral. This can offer a flow into of profits, in particular when you have a big following on social media or a blog. For instance, if you are a meals blogger and promote a kitchen appliance, you could earn passive profits from the partner price earned from the income made via your referral link.

In give up, there are numerous types of passive profits, every with its very own advantages and drawbacks. Understanding the distinct styles of passive profits will can help you understand which streams of profits may be appropriate for you. Rental earnings, dividend earnings, hobby earnings, royalty income, capital profits profits, and associate advertising and advertising and marketing earnings are all examples of passive profits streams that allow you to gain monetary freedom and independence. There are various kinds of passive income streams that you could create to reap economic freedom. Below are some examples:

Passive Income Type   Description   Example

Rental Income   Income generated from renting out property or belongings   Rental profits from actual assets or device

Dividend Income   Income generated from proudly proudly owning stocks or shares in a organization   Dividend earnings from stocks or stocks in a enterprise

Interest Income   Income generated from lending cash to others   Interest income from economic financial savings money owed, bonds, or peer-to-peer lending

Capital Gains   Income generated from selling an asset for greater than you paid for it   Selling a belongings or a stock at a profit

Affiliate Marketing   Income generated from selling extraordinary people's merchandise and earning a price   Earnings from selling products on a weblog or social media

Royalties   Income generated from the use of intellectual assets   Royalties from publishing a e-book or licensing a patent

Online Courses   Income generated from promoting on line courses or digital products   Earnings from promoting an internet route or e-book

It is essential to word that a few passive income streams require extra upfront funding or try than others. For example, condominium income requires an funding in property or assets, on the identical time as companion advertising may be started out with minimum investment. It is also essential to bear in mind the capability dangers and returns of every shape of passive profits movement earlier than making an investment time or money into them.

Ultimately, the shape of passive income flow which you select will rely upon your non-public desires and interests. Some human beings might also decide on the stability of rental income, while others can also moreover choose the potential for high returns thru making an investment in shares or developing digital products. Whatever the case may be, growing a various portfolio of passive income streams can assist make certain prolonged-term financial stability and fulfillment.

1. Three Myths and misconceptions approximately passive earnings

Passive income is frequently misunderstood, and there are numerous myths and misconceptions about it. In this monetary destroy, we are capable to speak some of the most common myths and misconceptions about passive earnings.

The first fable is that passive income is easy and calls for no strive. This isn't real. While passive income can offer a normal circulate of profits with out lively involvement, it despite the fact that calls for strive and art work in advance. For instance, if you want to generate passive earnings from condominium property, you want to invest time and money prematurely to buy the assets, keep it, and locate tenants.

The 2d fantasy is that passive income should make you rich rapid. This is also not actual. Passive earnings streams usually require time and effort to accumulate, and they will no longer offer large profits at the start. For instance, if you need to generate passive earnings from dividend shares, it is able to take years of consistent making an funding to build up a widespread portfolio that may provide large earnings.

The 0.33 fable is that passive earnings requires large quantities of cash to start. While having money to invest can assist, it is not crucial to generate passive earnings. For instance, if you need to generate passive profits from partner marketing, you could begin with a small net website or social media account and steadily boom your audience.

The fourth fantasy is that passive earnings isn't always taxable. This isn't real. Passive earnings remains taken into consideration earnings and is problem to taxation. For instance, in case you generate passive earnings from rental property, you can need to pay taxes on the apartment income.

The 5th fantasy is that passive profits is sincerely passive and calls for no control. While passive income streams also can require much less manage than energetic income streams, they despite the fact that require a few diploma of manage and tracking. For instance, if you generate passive income from dividend stocks, you want to display screen the overall overall performance of the shares and make changes as crucial.

In cease, passive earnings is regularly misunderstood, and there are numerous myths and misconceptions about it. Passive profits requires strive and paintings in advance, can also additionally take time to accumulate, does now not continuously require massive quantities of cash to begin, stays taxable, and calls for a few level of manage and monitoring. Understanding those myths and misconceptions let you growth sensible expectancies and construct a sustainable passive profits movement.

Chapter 2: Building A Strong Financial Foundation

In order to gain economic freedom and stay off passive income, it is vital to have a sturdy monetary foundation. This technique having a sturdy understanding of your finances and taking steps to ensure your economic protection. In this financial ruin, we're going to find out the significance of constructing a strong economic foundation and discuss a few sensible steps you could take to obtain economic protection.

Financial safety is essential for numerous reasons. First and primary, it gives a experience of balance and peace of mind. When you have have been given a solid financial foundation, you may climate sudden activities like undertaking loss or medical emergencies with out feeling crushed. This enjoy of safety can lessen pressure and tension and assist you to reputation on unique regions of your lifestyles.

Another vital cause to gather a strong financial basis is to attain lengthy-time period financial desires. Whether you need to retire early, begin your private business, or tour the arena, having a strong financial foundation may additionally need to make these dreams conceivable. By taking steps to shop coins, make investments because it ought to be, and manipulate your charge range successfully, you can create a roadmap for reaching your dreams.

So, how do you construct a sturdy financial foundation? The first step is to create a finances. This way taking an sincere have a look at your earnings and charges and developing a plan for the manner you may spend and preserve your coins. This may be a frightening mission, but it is crucial for records your price range and making sure you are at the right song.

Once you've got a fee variety in area, the next step is to construct an emergency fund. This is a monetary savings account that you may use to cover sudden costs like automobile safety or clinical bills. Ideally, your emergency fund should be massive sufficient to cover 3 to 6 months of living fees.

Investing is every different important part of building a sturdy economic foundation. While passive income can offer a steady motion of income, it's miles critical to do not forget that every one investments encompass some degree of risk. That's why it is crucial to make investments accurately and diversify your portfolio. This way spreading your investments all through numerous asset commands like shares, bonds, and actual property.

Finally, it's miles essential to control your debt efficaciously. While a few kinds of debt, like a loan, may be a extremely good investment, different types of debt, like credit score score score card debt, can be a exceptional drain on your rate range. Make a plan to pay off excessive-interest debt as quick as possible, and keep away from taking on new debt each time viable.

In this financial ruin, we've explored the significance of building a robust monetary basis and mentioned some practical steps you may take to collect financial protection. By developing a fee range, building an emergency fund, making an funding successfully, and managing your debt efficiently, you may create a robust foundation for conducting your economic goals and residing off passive income. Remember, financial protection isn't just about having extra money – it is about having greater peace of mind and the liberty to pursue the existence you need.

2.1 Understanding your modern monetary scenario

Before you can begin constructing a robust monetary foundation, it is critical to apprehend your cutting-edge economic scenario. This consists of reading your profits, prices, debts, and belongings.

To start, you have to calculate your month-to-month profits. This includes your revenue, any bonuses or commissions, and any more property of earnings. Next, you need to decide your monthly prices. This consists of all of your constant prices, which encompass lease or loan bills, car payments, coverage, and utilities. You have to moreover account to your variable fees, consisting of groceries, entertainment, and excursion.

Once you've got calculated your earnings and prices, you could determine your monthly coins glide. If your charges are greater than your profits, you may be living beyond your approach and accumulating debt. However, if your income is more than your prices, you have got a amazing cash go along with the drift and might use the more money to pay off debt or make investments for the future.

It is likewise essential to investigate your money owed. This consists of credit score card debt, pupil loans, car loans, and every other excellent loans. You need to decide the full quantity of debt you owe, the hobby fees, and the month-to-month bills. By doing so, you may prioritize paying off your money owed and keep away from amassing more debt in the destiny.

Another detail of know-how your cutting-edge economic scenario is assessing your home. This consists of any investments, retirement bills, real assets, and specific valuable possessions. By identifying your internet worth, you may benefit a higher facts of your monetary health and grow to be privy to areas for improvement.

In addition to analyzing your income, costs, money owed, and assets, it is vital to remember your financial goals. What do you choice to achieve collectively along with your money? Do you want to keep for retirement, purchase a domestic, or adventure the area? By identifying your economic dreams, you could create a plan to benefit them.

In the desk beneath, we've got got supplied a template for reading your modern-day-day monetary state of affairs. By filling out this template, you can benefit a higher expertise of your monetary fitness and discover areas for improvement.

Category	Amount
Monthly Income	[insert amount]
Fixed Expenses	[insert amount]
Variable Expenses	[insert amount]
Monthly Cash Flow	[insert amount]
Total Debt	[insert amount]
Interest Rates	[insert rates]
Monthly Payments	[insert payments]
Total Assets	[insert amount]
Net Worth	[insert amount]
Financial Goals	[insert goals]

In end, information your contemporary-day monetary situation is step one in building a strong monetary foundation. By studying your income, prices, debts, belongings, and economic goals, you may create a plan to achieve economic freedom and safety. Whether your intention is to live off passive earnings, give up your system, or gain greater economic and personal security for your lifestyles, all of it begins offevolved with information your current-day financial scenario.

2.2 Creating a price range and managing expenses

Creating a price range and managing charges is a vital detail of building a robust financial foundation. A price variety is largely a plan that permits you allocate your income in the path of wonderful fees, which incorporates rent, groceries, transportation, and entertainment. By growing a price range and tracking your costs, you may benefit higher manipulate over your rate range and avoid overspending.

To begin developing a price variety, you have to first choose out your income and charges.

This includes your monthly earnings, similarly in your consistent and variable charges. You can use the template provided within the preceding paragraph to help you with this manner.

Once you have got were given identified your earnings and fees, you can start allocating your earnings toward one among a kind classes. You need to prioritize your costs primarily based on their importance, with crucial charges collectively with rent and utilities taking priority over discretionary fees together with amusement and excursion.

It is vital to make sure that your charges do now not exceed your earnings. If you discover which you are overspending, you may need to cut back on effective charges or find out methods to increase your earnings. For instance, you could look for strategies to lessen your utility bills or negotiate a lift at artwork.

Managing your fees is also an vital difficulty of making a finances. This includes tracking your expenses and ensuring that you are staying interior your price variety. You can use a spreadsheet or a budgeting app to help you keep music of your charges.

It is likewise critical to study your finances regularly and make changes as crucial. For instance, in case you discover that you are constantly overspending in a great class, you can want to adjust your price range to reduce your fees in that beauty.

In addition to growing a finances and handling your fees, there are unique techniques that you can use to shop cash and beautify your economic fitness. For example, you may look for strategies to reduce your debt, collectively with by means of consolidating your loans or negotiating a lower hobby charge.

You can also search for strategies to boom your earnings, which includes by manner of beginning a element corporation or freelancing. By developing your profits, you cannot best beautify your economic fitness, however moreover create new possibilities for yourself.

In prevent, developing a budget and handling your fees is a essential factor of building a robust monetary basis. By prioritizing your fees, monitoring your spending, and making changes as vital, you may advantage higher control over your budget and avoid overspending. Whether your cause is to live off passive earnings, end your activity, or advantage extra monetary and private safety on your lifestyles, it all starts offevolved offevolved with developing a price range and coping with your fees.

In the table beneath, we've got provided a template for growing a charge range. By the usage of this template, you can create a finances this is tailored to your profits and fees and make sure that your charges are in keeping with your financial goals.

Category	Budgeted Amount	Actual Amount
Housing	[insert amount]	[insert amount]

Utilities   [insert amount]   [insert amount]

Transportation   [insert amount]   [insert amount]

Groceries   [insert amount]   [insert amount]

Entertainment   [insert amount]   [insert amount]

Travel   [insert amount]   [insert amount]

Miscellaneous   [insert amount]   [insert amount]

Total Expenses   [insert amount]   [insert amount]

Income   [insert amount]   [insert amount]

Cash Flow   [insert amount]   [insert amount]

In cease, growing a price range and handling prices is vital for constructing a strong economic foundation. By analyzing your charges, developing a finances, and managing your expenses successfully, you could make certain that your charges are in line with your profits and economic dreams.

2.Three Reducing debt and growing monetary savings

Building a robust monetary basis involves key components: reducing debt and growing financial financial savings. These two standards cross hand-in-hand and can help you attain financial freedom in the end. In this bankruptcy, we're able to talk sensible methods to perform each.

Let's start with decreasing debt. One of the best strategies to cope with debt is through developing a fee range. A fee variety enables you select out your income and charges and lets in you to appearance in which your cash is going. Once you have got a clean image of your budget, you could select out regions in which you can lessen once more on expenses and redirect the ones finances closer to paying off debt.

Another method for lowering debt is to attention on paying off excessive-interest debt first. High-hobby debt, together with credit rating score card debt, can brief spiral out of control if left unchecked. By prioritizing those debts, you can store your self a large amount of coins in interest charges over the years.

Now allow's communicate about developing financial savings. Building up your monetary economic financial savings is important for reaching economic protection. One of the brilliant strategies to growth your monetary financial savings is thru installing computerized financial savings contributions. By automating your savings, you may now not even want to reflect onconsideration on putting cash aside every month - it's going to display up mechanically.

Another method for growing financial monetary financial savings is with the resource of developing a economic financial savings plan. This plan need to define your short-time period and lengthy-term financial savings dreams, further to the steps you want to take to accumulate the ones dreams. For instance, in case your intention is to buy a down fee on a domestic, you can want to determine how lots you want to store every month and the way long it'll take to attain your purpose.

To further illustrate the relationship amongst debt reduce price and economic savings, allow's have a have a observe the subsequent table:

Debt Reduction	Savings Increase
Creating a budget	Automatic savings contributions
Prioritizing immoderate-interest debt	Creating a financial financial savings plan
Negotiating decrease interest charges	Investing in a retirement account
Consolidating debt	Investing in a immoderate-yield savings account

As you may see, the ones strategies paintings collectively that will help you gather your economic dreams. By decreasing your debt, you free up extra cash to place towards financial savings. And through way of increasing your financial savings, you can have a economic cushion to fall back on in case of emergencies, in addition to the belongings you need to gather your long-time period economic dreams.

In end, lowering debt and growing financial savings are essential additives of building a sturdy monetary basis. By imposing the techniques referred to on this financial disaster, you may be nicely in your manner to accomplishing financial freedom and safety. Remember, it is in no way too overdue to begin taking control of your charge range, so do now not wait - start in recent times!

In conclusion, constructing a sturdy financial foundation is vital for conducting passive earnings success. It units the degree for growing a stable monetary plan, lowering debt, and putting in wholesome financial behavior if you want to very last an entire life. By imposing the techniques discussed in this bankruptcy, you may start taking manipulate of your finances and flow inside the route of financial freedom. Remember that monetary protection is not pretty lots amassing wealth, however it's also approximately having peace of mind and being capable of climate economic storms that can come your manner.

By growing a strong monetary basis, you may make certain that you are organized for any disturbing situations that come your way and function the property to take benefit of opportunities for generating passive income. Additionally, a sturdy economic foundation presents the stability needed to weather economic crises, which embody the ultra-modern COVID-19 pandemic, which could significantly effect non-public budget.

Chapter 3: Investing For Passive Income

Investing for passive profits is a critical step in the direction of attaining monetary freedom. When you invest your cash correctly, it is able to generate income for you with out requiring lively attempt to your detail. This profits, called passive profits, can offer you with the financial protection and flexibility had to pursue your passions, tour, or spend more time with loved ones. In this bankruptcy, we are succesful to talk about the electricity of creating an investment and the techniques you can use to start producing passive income.

Investing may be a powerful device for carrying out your monetary dreams. By setting your money to be actually right for you, you may generate earnings, construct wealth, and gain lengthy-term economic safety. However, making an funding additionally may be intimidating, especially for people who are new to the arena of finance. With such a lot of investment alternatives available, it is able to be hard to recognise in which to start.

That's in which this financial ruin is available in. We will offer you with a realistic guide to making an funding for passive earnings, which includes the remarkable types of investments available, the way to choose out the proper investments in your dreams, and strategies for minimizing danger and maximizing returns. We can even communicate the blessings and disadvantages of numerous funding options, which includes stocks, bonds, and real assets, to help you make informed options approximately wherein to make investments your coins.

One of the most high-quality advantages of creating an funding is the energy of compound hobby. When you make investments your coins, it could earn interest, dividends, or unique varieties of profits. Over time, this profits can generate even more earnings, developing a snowball effect that could significantly growth your wealth. The in advance you start making an investment, the extra time your investments want to compound and expand, making it much less tough to acquire your monetary goals.

Investing moreover lets in you to diversify your portfolio, spreading your coins at some point of one in all a kind assets and decreasing the danger of losing the whole lot in a unmarried investment. By diversifying your portfolio, you may protect your investments from market fluctuations and create a greater strong deliver of passive income.

In conclusion, making an investment is a effective tool for generating passive profits and achieving financial freedom. By investing correctly, you can build wealth, create a strong deliver of earnings, and gain the monetary security needed to pursue your passions and live the existence you want. In the following chapters, we can delve deeper into the unique types of investments to be had and offer you with practical strategies for constructing a passive profits motion through making an investment.

three.1 Types of investments for passive income

Investing for passive income is an notable manner to generate a normal flow into of coins go with the flow with out actively running for it. There are diverse kinds of investments that you can make to earn passive profits, and on this economic disaster, we will find out some of the maximum famous options.

The first type of funding for passive profits is dividend stocks. Dividend stocks are shares in organizations that pay out a issue of their profits to shareholders inside the shape of dividends. By making an investment in dividend-paying stocks, you could earn a regular movement of passive earnings on the equal time as no longer having to sell your stocks.

Another famous funding opportunity for passive earnings is real belongings. Real assets can provide a robust supply of passive earnings via condominium earnings. You can spend money on condo homes and gather month-to-month lease bills from tenants. Alternatively, you may spend money on real estate investment trusts (REITs), that are businesses that private and manage earnings-generating real belongings homes.

Peer-to-peer lending is each other shape of funding which can generate passive profits. In peer-to-peer lending, you lend cash to humans or organizations via an internet platform. These borrowers then pay off the loan with hobby, presenting you with a deliver of passive profits.

Next on the list is bonds. Bonds are debt securities which is probably issued through companies, governments, or one of a kind groups. By making an funding in bonds, you could earn a everyday go along with the go with the flow of passive income in the form of hobby bills.

Finally, there are exchange-traded finances (ETFs) and mutual rate range. ETFs and mutual price range are funding cars that pool cash from multiple traders to put money into a severa portfolio of belongings. By making an funding in ETFs or mutual price variety, you can earn passive profits via dividends or hobby bills.

To further illustrate the specific sorts of investments for passive income, allow's have a examine the subsequent table:

Investment Type   Description   Example

Dividend stocks   Shares in agencies that pay out a element of their income to shareholders within the shape of dividends   Johnson & Johnson (JNJ)

Real property   Investment in condo houses or actual property investment trusts (REITs)   Realty Income Corporation (O)

Peer-to-peer lending   Lending coins to individuals or businesses thru a web platform Lending Club (LC)

Bonds   Debt securities which are issued via corporations, governments, or different companies   US Treasury Bonds

ETFs/mutual price range   Investment automobiles that pool cash from more than one traders to invest in a various portfolio of property   Vanguard Total Stock Market ETF (VTI)

It's important to be aware that each of those investment sorts includes its very very very own set of risks and rewards. Therefore, it is essential to do your research and understand the dangers related to every investment in advance than you make a decision. Additionally, diversification is high on the subject of making an funding for passive income. By spreading your investments in the course of multiple asset instructions, you can restriction your hazard and maximize your capability returns.

In end, there are various forms of investments to be had for producing passive income. Whether you pick out out to put money into dividend shares, actual assets, peer-to-peer lending, bonds, or ETFs/mutual budget, it's miles critical to understand the dangers and rewards associated with each investment. With cautious research and proper diversification, making an funding for passive profits can offer you with a consistent waft of cash go along with the waft and assist you reap financial freedom.

three.2 Risk vs reward

Investing for passive profits may be an first-rate manner to assemble wealth and benefit economic freedom, but it is essential to apprehend the connection among hazard and praise. The first-rate rule of making an investment is that the better the capability reward, the higher the threat. In this monetary disaster, we are able to explore the idea of hazard vs. Reward and the way to balance the 2 even as making an investment for passive income.

Let's begin by using defining danger. Risk refers back to the probability of dropping coins on an funding. All investments consist of a few diploma of chance, and it's far vital to understand the dangers related to each funding earlier than you decide.

On the alternative hand, reward refers back to the ability cross again on an investment. The better the capability bypass returned, the more attractive the investment can be.

To similarly illustrate the connection among hazard and reward, allow's take a look at the following table:

Investment Type	Potential Reward	Potential Risk
Dividend stocks	High	Low
Real property	High	Medium to High
Peer-to-peer lending	Medium to High	Medium to High

Bonds   Low to Medium   Low to Medium

ETFs/mutual price range   Medium   Medium

As you could see, every funding type has a fantastic potential praise and potential hazard. Dividend shares are taken into consideration a low-threat funding with a immoderate capability praise, at the same time as real belongings consists of a medium to excessive degree of danger with a high functionality reward.

When it involves balancing hazard vs. Reward, it is vital to recognize your funding dreams and threat tolerance. If you are seeking out a steady motion of passive income with low chance, dividend shares may be the right desire for you. However, if you're inclined to tackle extra danger for a better potential reward, real property or peer-to-peer lending can be extra suitable.

It's essential to be aware that diversification is essential almost about balancing risk vs. Reward. By spreading your investments all through multiple asset training, you could lower your hazard and maximize your potential returns.

In stop, making an investment for passive profits calls for a cautious balance amongst threat and praise. While better functionality rewards may be attractive, they regularly encompass a higher degree of risk. By information your investment desires and chance tolerance and diversifying your investments, you could bring together a portfolio that generates a consistent move of passive income at the equal time as minimizing your risk.

three.Three Strategies for a hit making an investment

Investing for passive earnings may be a rewarding way to construct wealth and reap economic freedom, however it's essential to have a technique in place to make sure your achievement. In this financial disaster, we can discover a few key strategies for a fulfillment investing for passive earnings.

Set funding goals: Before you begin making an funding, it is essential to set smooth funding goals. What do you need to gather thru your investments? Are you seeking out lengthy-term boom or short-term income? How plenty danger are you willing to address? By answering those questions and setting precise investment dreams, you could create a plan that aligns together together with your financial dreams.

Diversify your portfolio: One of the most important techniques for a success making an funding is diversification. By spreading your investments for the duration of unique asset commands and industries, you may lessen your hazard and maximize your functionality returns. A properly-brilliant portfolio can also consist of a combination of stocks, bonds, real belongings, and one of a kind assets.

Invest for the prolonged-term: Investing for passive earnings is a marathon, not a dash. It's critical to have an extended-term attitude and keep away from making impulsive options based totally definitely mostly on quick-time period market fluctuations. By making an funding for the prolonged-term, you could take gain of compounding returns and build wealth over the years.

Consider tax implications: When investing for passive profits, it's miles crucial to undergo in mind the tax implications of your investments. Certain investments, which encompass actual property or municipal bonds, can also offer tax benefits that allow you to preserve more of your profits.

Keep an eye fixed fixed on charges: Fees can consume into your investment returns over the years, so it's miles essential to keep a watch fixed at the charges associated with your investments. Look for low-charge funding options, which incorporates index budget or ETFs, and keep away from excessive-fee investments which can erode your returns.

Let's test the subsequent table to look how the ones strategies can be implemented to awesome sorts of investments:

Investment Type	Investment Goals	Diversification	Long-time period Perspective	Tax Implications	Fee Consciousness
Dividend shares	Income technology	Spread investments at some stage in sectors	Hold for the prolonged-term	Consider tax implications of dividend income	Look for low-fee index fee range
Real property	Income generation and appreciation	Diversify at some point of geographies and belongings sorts	Hold for the lengthy-time period	Consider tax benefits of real property investment	Keep a watch on assets control charges
Peer-to-peer lending	High returns with a few threat	Diversify in the course of borrowers and loan kinds	Hold for the prolonged-time period	Consider tax implications of hobby earnings	Look for systems with low prices

Bonds   Income generation and balance Diversify throughout issuers and maturities Hold for the long-time period   Consider tax implications of interest income   Look for low-rate bond price range

ETFs/mutual finances   Balanced increase and profits   Diversify during asset instructions and sectors   Hold for the lengthy-time period Consider tax implications of capital earnings Look for low-rate index price variety

By applying those strategies on your investments, you may create a well-rounded portfolio that generates a regular circulate of passive profits and permits you purchased your economic goals.

In quit, making an investment for passive income can be a powerful tool for accomplishing financial freedom and protection. By cautiously choosing and diversifying investments, individuals can create a reliable drift of passive earnings that could useful aid their life-style and assist them attain their economic goals. The power of making an investment lies in its ability to generate wealth through the years via compounding returns and the capacity for capital appreciation.

However, it's miles vital to approach making an investment with a nicely-planned investment portfolio that takes into interest person economic desires, hazard tolerance, and time horizon. A well-planned funding portfolio can provide a balanced blend of asset training and investment strategies that artwork together to benefit financial dreams. It also can help mitigate risks with the useful resource of diversifying throughout exquisite sorts of investments and spreading out investment capital.

Chapter 4: Real Estate Investing

Welcome to Chapter 4, in which we are capable of find out the thrilling global of actual property making an investment. Real assets is a tried and real technique of generating passive earnings and building wealth over the long time. Many a achievement shoppers have built their fortunes thru actual estate investments, and it's far a way this is available to people of all profits degrees.

Real belongings making an investment is the method of buying, proudly proudly owning, handling, renting, or promoting property for earnings. It can take many exceptional office work, from investing in single-family houses to business houses like office houses or retail regions. The benefits of actual belongings investing are severa, at the side of the ability for coins go with the drift, appreciation, tax blessings, and leverage.

One of the maximum tremendous benefits of actual assets making an investment is the functionality for passive income. When you personal a condominium property, you could generate profits from condo payments that exceed your charges, which embody loan payments, property taxes, and protection charges. This can provide a reliable supply of income that requires minimum attempt to your thing, specially if you lease a belongings management industrial employer employer to address every day operations.

Another advantage of actual assets making an funding is the capacity for appreciation. Over time, real belongings values have a tendency to growth, supplying an opportunity for buyers to earn a profits after they promote the assets. Additionally, actual belongings gives severa tax blessings, which include deductions for mortgage hobby, belongings taxes, and depreciation.

Finally, actual belongings making an funding allows for leverage, meaning that clients can purchase assets with borrowed cash, likely developing their returns. This may be particularly extremely good in a low-interest-price environment, in which borrowing charges are low.

In this economic catastrophe, we are capable of dive deeper into the benefits of actual assets making an investment, the special forms of homes available for investment, and the techniques for maximizing your returns. Whether you're a seasoned investor or clearly starting, real estate making an funding is a powerful device for sporting out economic freedom thru passive income.

four.1 Types of real assets investments

Real property making an funding may be a terrific manner to generate passive income and build lengthy-term wealth. However, there are certainly one of a kind sorts of real estate investments that possible make, each with its private blessings and disadvantages.

One type of actual assets investment is rental homes. These are houses which are supplied with the purpose of renting them out to tenants. Rental houses may be each residential or business and may variety from unmarried-family homes to apartment complexes. The earnings generated from condominium residences comes from the rent paid with the aid of tenants, and the charge of the assets can appreciate over time. However, rental homes also can encompass expenses which include protection and repair costs, assets management prices, and vacancies.

Another form of real belongings investment is real assets investment trusts (REITs). REITs are companies that personal and manage income-generating residences consisting of office houses, condominium complexes, and buying centers. Investing in a REIT allows humans to private a element of these houses with out honestly proudly owning the assets outright. REITs can provide diversification and liquidity, as they may be publicly traded on inventory exchanges. However, they will moreover embody manage prices and decrease returns than direct real belongings investments.

Real property crowdfunding is a enormously new form of investment that allows people to invest in real belongings projects along different customers. Through on line structures, human beings can put money into particular real assets duties with as low as some hundred greenbacks. Real assets crowdfunding can provide diversification and the capability to invest in unique duties, but it additionally comes with risks collectively with lack of liquidity and the potential for fraud.

Finally, flipping houses is some other form of real property funding that is composed of buying a assets with the aim of solving it up and reselling it for a profits. Flipping homes may be profitable, however it furthermore comes with dangers which incorporates surprising upkeep and market fluctuations.

The following table summarizes the advantages and drawbacks of each form of real property investment:

Type of Real Estate Investment   Advantages   Disadvantages

Rental Properties   Passive income, belongings appreciation   Expenses collectively with upkeep and renovation, vacancies

REITs   Diversification, liquidity   Management prices, lower returns than direct actual property investments

Real Estate Crowdfunding   Diversification, capability to invest in precise responsibilities Lack of liquidity, capacity for fraud

Flipping Houses   Potential for immoderate earnings   Unexpected renovation, marketplace fluctuations

When deciding on a kind of real belongings investment, it is important to keep in mind one's economic desires, risk tolerance, and personal alternatives. It is also critical to do thorough studies and are searching for the recommendation of specialists together with actual assets stores, prison specialists, and economic advisors. By cautiously considering the advantages and disadvantages of each kind of real estate funding, human beings can also want to make knowledgeable alternatives and gather a a fulfillment real property portfolio.

four.2 Finding and evaluating residences

Once you have got decided to spend money on real property, the following step is locating and comparing residences. There are severa strategies to discover capacity investment homes, which consist of on-line listings, operating with a actual belongings agent, attending auctions or tax income, and networking with different customers. It's important to do your due diligence and punctiliously research any assets in advance than making an offer.

One critical component to bear in mind whilst comparing a property is its area. A belongings's location can drastically have an effect on its fee and capability for apartment profits. Consider factors which incorporates proximity to schools, transportation, shopping for centers, and one-of-a-kind facilities that tenants also can fee.

Another component to don't forget is the situation of the assets. A belongings that calls for massive protection or renovations won't be properly without a doubt well worth the funding, as those expenses can quickly add up and decrease into your capability profits. It's crucial to have a thorough inspection of the property finished thru a expert to recognize any capability issues.

In addition to the property itself, it is vital to preserve in thoughts the community marketplace situations. Are assets values developing or decreasing? Is there a immoderate demand for condominium homes in the area? These factors can appreciably effect the capability pass returned on investment.

When evaluating a belongings, it is also crucial to take into account the financing options available to you. Will you be paying in cash, or will you want to stable a mortgage? It's essential to analyze specific lenders and mortgage options to discover the incredible healthful to your monetary situation.

Overall, locating and comparing residences is a critical step in a success actual estate making an investment. Taking the time to thoroughly research and evaluate functionality homes will assist you to make informed investment alternatives and growth your probabilities of accomplishing your monetary dreams.

four.Three Financing options for real belongings making an funding

When it comes to actual estate making an funding, financing is an crucial consideration. There are numerous financing alternatives available to investors, each with their personal blessings and downsides. The maximum commonplace financing alternatives for actual belongings making an investment encompass:

Conventional Mortgages: A traditional mortgage is a loan supplied via a economic corporation or great monetary corporation to buy a assets. These loans normally require a down charge of at the least 20% and feature constant interest prices.

FHA Loans: An FHA loan is a government-subsidized loan this is designed to assist humans with lower credit rating score ratings or smaller down payments purchase a domestic. These loans require a down rate of 3.Five% and feature extra bendy credit score score score requirements.

Hard Money Loans: Hard coins loans are short-term loans which can be usually used for repair-and-turn houses. These loans are generally provided through non-public lenders and function higher hobby quotes and charges than conventional mortgages.

Private Money Loans: Private coins loans are similar to difficult cash loans, but they may be furnished with the aid of human beings in choice to personal creditors. These loans often have more bendy terms than difficult cash loans.

Home Equity Loans: Home fairness loans assist you to borrow inside the route of the equity to your contemporary domestic to buy an investment property. These loans regularly have lower hobby charges than one-of-a-type varieties of loans, but they require you to have a substantial quantity of fairness in your house.

Seller Financing: With company financing, the seller of the property gives financing to the purchaser. This may be a terrific alternative for buyers who've problem qualifying for conventional loans.

It is important to evaluate the financing options to be had to you and pick out out the most effective that extraordinary suits your investment strategy and monetary state of affairs. Consider factors including hobby expenses, costs, down fee requirements, and repayment phrases. It is likewise crucial to have a sturdy statistics of your funding goals and the manner the financing will impact your trendy monetary plan.

Financing Option	Description	Pros	Cons
Conventional Mortgage	A conventional home loan furnished by means of a financial employer or other monetary organization	Low hobby fees; predictable monthly bills	Requires a high credit rating and huge down price; can be tough to qualify for
FHA Loan	A authorities-sponsored loan designed to assist low-earnings and number one-time homebuyers	Low down price requirements; lower credit rating necessities	Requires loan coverage fees; assets want to meet excessive satisfactory eligibility standards
Hard Money Loan	A short-term mortgage commonly used by real property buyers to finance repair-and-flip initiatives	Quick funding; a whole lot much less emphasis on credit rating score	High hobby prices; calls for a wonderful down rate; short repayment terms

Private Money Loan   A mortgage from a private person or organization in place of a conventional economic institution   Flexible phrases; may be simpler to qualify for   May require a better hobby charge; a whole lot plenty much less regulation and oversight

HELOC   A domestic fairness line of credit score score rating that allows owners to borrow towards the fairness of their domestic Low hobby costs; flexibility in how finances are used   Requires a immoderate credit score score rating and wonderful fairness within the assets; variable hobby costs can result in unpredictable month-to-month payments

It's essential to thoroughly research and hold in thoughts all financing options earlier than you decide, as each preference has its very private benefits and disadvantages.

In conclusion, real assets making an funding is an attractive desire for those seeking out passive profits due to its many blessings. Not best does it provide the capacity for a normal circulate of income, but it additionally offers the possibility for lengthy-term appreciation and fairness growth. Additionally, real assets making an funding can be a shape of diversification for parents that could also have a majority of their wealth tied up in stocks and bonds.

However, it's miles essential to word that real assets investing is not without its dangers. It calls for cautious studies and due diligence to make sure that a property is a valid funding, and there can be surprising costs or emptiness intervals that can effect cash go with the flow.

Despite those capability disturbing situations, real belongings making an investment may be a powerful tool for producing passive income and constructing prolonged-time period wealth. By building a numerous portfolio of houses and staying on top of market traits and changes, investors can probably create a steady flow of income that can offer economic security and freedom.

In prevent, actual property making an investment can provide awesome functionality for passive earnings, but it requires a thoughtful and strategic approach to maximize its blessings. As with any funding, it is critical to weigh the dangers and rewards and to have a well-deliberate approach in vicinity to achieve fulfillment. With careful making plans and manage, actual belongings making an investment may be a precious addition to a passive earnings portfolio.

Chapter 5: Stock Market Investing

Welcome to Chapter 5 of "Transform Your Life: Living off Passive Income, Quitting Your Job, and Achieving Financial Freedom." In this financial ruin, we can be discussing inventory market making an funding, a subject that is frequently seen as complex and intimidating, but may be very profitable while finished correctly.

At its center, stock market making an investment entails attempting to find and promoting shares of publicly-traded groups, with the cause of generating a profit. This may be completed thru a number of techniques, consisting of price investing, increase making an investment, and dividend making an investment, among others. While those techniques range in their specifics, all of them rely on the same number one principle: figuring out organizations which can be probable to develop in price over time, and searching for shares in those businesses in the hopes of taking advantage of that increase.

Of route, inventory market investing isn't always with out its dangers. The stock marketplace can be volatile, and costs can range all of sudden in response to a large variety of factors, from macroeconomic trends to business enterprise-unique news. As a cease result, it's far essential to technique stock market making an funding with a clean plan and an extended-time period mind-set. This means doing all your research, diversifying your portfolio, and maintaining off the temptation to chase quick earnings or look at marketplace hype.

In this financial ruin, we will find out the basics of stock market making an investment, from statistics how the inventory market works to developing a valid investment method. We can even study some of the maximum common errors that investors make even as investing in the inventory marketplace, and a way to keep away from them. By the save you of this bankruptcy, you want to have a solid knowledge of what it takes to make investments effectively inside the inventory marketplace and begin building a strong basis to your passive earnings go with the flow.

five.1 Types of stocks and investments

When it includes making an funding inside the stock marketplace, there are numerous sorts of shares and investments to don't forget.

The maximum not unusual form of stock is a common stock, which represents possession in a organisation and offers shareholders the proper to vote on corporate alternatives.

Another kind of stock is a desired stock, which usually can pay a tough and rapid dividend and has priority over not unusual inventory within the event of a enterprise's liquidation. In addition to individual stocks, investors can also spend money on change-traded price variety (ETFs) and mutual finances. ETFs are much like mutual budget in that they pool together shoppers' coins to spend money on a diverse portfolio of belongings, but they're traded on inventory exchanges like person shares.

Mutual fee range, alternatively, are controlled through expert portfolio managers who make investments the finances' assets in some of securities, along with stocks and bonds. Some consumers additionally select to spend money on index price variety, which may be designed to tune the overall performance of a specific market index, consisting of the S&P 500.

Another well-known investment choice is bonds, that are debt securities issued by way of organizations or governments. Bonds commonly offer a difficult and rapid price of go back and are taken into consideration an awful lot much less risky than shares. However, they will offer lower returns than shares over the long time.

Overall, the important thing to a achievement inventory market making an funding is to have a well-various portfolio that consists of a mixture of shares, bonds, and different investment cars. By spreading your investments throughout particular styles of belongings, you could help lessen your danger and potentially maximize your returns.

Type of Investment   Characteristics

Blue-Chip Stocks   Large, properly-set up corporations with a long facts of fulfillment and balance. Often pay dividends.

Growth Stocks   Smaller, speedy-developing businesses with functionality for immoderate returns however furthermore higher hazard. Typically reinvest earnings instead of paying dividends.

Value Stocks   Underpriced shares which may be believed to have robust functionality for growth in the destiny. Can be loads much less unstable than growth shares.

Income Stocks   Stocks that pay excessive dividends and offer a constant motion of profits. Often in greater stable industries which include utilities or actual estate.

Index Funds   A sort of mutual fund that tracks a particular marketplace index, collectively with the S&P 500. Offers diversification and generally has decrease prices.

Exchange-Traded Funds (ETFs)   Similar to index price variety, but may be supplied and provided like person stocks. Often have decrease costs than mutual price range.

Bonds   A form of debt protection that offers a fixed rate of pass again over a hard and fast period of time. Generally considered plenty much less unstable than stocks, however moreover typically provide lower returns.

Options   Contracts that deliver investors the right to shop for or sell an asset at a selected fee inner a fixed time body. Can be used for hypothesis or hedging.

Futures   Contracts that require shoppers to buy or promote an asset at a selected price on a tough and fast future date. Often used for hedging in opposition to charge fluctuations.

This isn't an exhaustive listing, but it covers some of the maximum commonplace styles of investments within the inventory market. It's critical to recollect that each shape of funding contains its very very own precise risks and capability rewards, and customers have to cautiously do not forget their dreams and danger tolerance in advance than making any investment selections.

five.2 Evaluating and selecting shares

Once you've got an know-how of the awesome types of stocks and investment alternatives available, the following step is to evaluate and pick out out out which stocks to invest in. This device requires studies, assessment, and a piece of intuition. The first step is to determine your investment desires and risk tolerance. This will guide your choice-making technique and help you come to be privy to the types of shares that align collectively together with your investment goals. Once you've got had been given diagnosed your funding desires, you may start studying character shares and analyzing their typical performance.

One critical element to preserve in thoughts on the identical time as evaluating stocks is their monetary health. This consists of reading their balance sheets, profits statements, and coins go along with the glide statements. You can also examine their profitability, profits increase, and debt tiers to determine their economic stability. Additionally, it's far vital to assess the business commercial enterprise corporation's management agency and their song document of handing over outcomes.

Another detail to bear in mind at the same time as evaluating shares is their business enterprise and marketplace dispositions. This consists of analyzing the overall market tendencies and identifying industries which might be expected to make bigger or decline inside the destiny. It's vital to test the organization's aggressive advantages and have a look at whether or not they are placed to take benefit of company dispositions.

Technical evaluation is likewise an crucial device to assess shares. This consists of looking on the stock's ancient fee and quantity records to understand styles and developments. Technical evaluation will let you decide the inventory's potential destiny regular overall performance and become privy to most efficient entry and go out elements.

When choosing shares to invest in, it is important to diversify your portfolio in the route of 1-of-a-type industries and sectors. This permits lessen hazard and ensures that your portfolio is not overly reliant on a single stock or enterprise. You also can recollect making an investment in index finances or trade-traded finances (ETFs) to benefit publicity to a various form of shares.

In cease, evaluating and choosing shares requires an intensive information of the wonderful kinds of stocks and investment alternatives to be had, as well as a whole evaluation of the stock's monetary fitness, enterprise trends, and technical overall performance. It's vital to diversify your portfolio and align your investments along with your funding dreams and hazard tolerance.

Metric Definition

P/E Ratio Price-to-income ratio: the inventory rate divided by way of way of the company's profits in keeping with percent (EPS) during the last twelve months. A immoderate P/E ratio can also mean that the stock is overrated, on the identical time as a low P/E ratio may also moreover advocate that it's far undervalued.

EPS Earnings constant with proportion: the enterprise's internet income divided with the useful resource of the full amount of extremely good shares. A better EPS shows that the commercial enterprise organisation is producing more income according to percentage, which might also make the stock extra appealing to customers.

Dividend Yield   The annual dividend charge according to percentage divided through the inventory rate. A better dividend yield may additionally make the stock greater appealing to earnings-searching out consumers.

P/B Ratio   Price-to-e-book ratio: the inventory charge divided via the business enterprise's e-book rate constant with percentage (belongings minus liabilities divided with the aid of manner of excellent shares). A low P/B ratio may also additionally propose that the inventory is undervalued relative to its property.

Market Cap   Market capitalization: the whole fee of all super shares of the enterprise's stock. This can supply customers an idea of the enterprise's duration and may be used to have a look at it to competition or the general marketplace.

Of course, this isn't always an exhaustive listing of all of the metrics that buyers can use to assess shares, but it could be a useful area to start. Investors must additionally maintain in thoughts factors similar to the employer's enterprise, manage group, and growth capability, amongst others, whilst making investment picks.

5.Three Portfolio diversification techniques

Portfolio diversification is a crucial technique as regards to making an investment in the stock market. It includes spreading your investments during quite a few numerous companies, industries, and asset instructions which will limit chance and maximize returns. By diversifying your portfolio, you can reduce the effect of any person funding to your fashionable portfolio standard typical performance.

One of the most effective techniques to diversify your portfolio is thru making an funding in index price range or trade-traded rate variety (ETFs). These price range music a specific market index, which includes the S&P 500, and offer exposure to a substantial kind of organizations and industries. By making an funding in a single fund, you may gain publicity to masses or maybe loads of corporations, greatly lowering your hazard of loss.

Another technique for portfolio diversification is making an investment in exceptional asset training. For instance, further to stocks, you may moreover spend money on bonds, real property, or commodities. Each of these asset commands has precise threat and cross decrease again tendencies, so via making an funding in a combination of them, you could create a extra balanced and severa portfolio.

It's additionally crucial to undergo in mind diversification interior person asset education. For instance, if you put money into shares, you have to hold in mind diversifying throughout top notch industries and sectors. This will help you avoid being too heavily uncovered to a person enterprise, together with technology or electricity, that may go through a downturn.

Finally, it is important to frequently assessment and rebalance your portfolio to make certain that it stays numerous. As a few investments can also perform higher than others over time, your portfolio may additionally come to be unbalanced if you do not regularly alter your holdings. By regularly reviewing and rebalancing your portfolio, you may ensure that it remains aligned collectively with your funding goals and chance tolerance.

In precis, portfolio diversification is a crucial thing of a success stock marketplace making an funding. By spreading your investments during pretty a number corporations, industries, and asset training, you could lower chance and maximize returns over the long term. Whether you pick out out to spend money on index price range, one-of-a-type asset training, or diversify interior person asset commands, the key is to create a balanced and numerous portfolio that aligns together along with your investment desires and chance tolerance.

Here is an instance of a various inventory portfolio:

Company	Industry	Market Cap	Allocation
Apple	Technology	Large-Cap	20%
Johnson & Johnson	Healthcare	Large-Cap	15%
Visa	Financial Services	Large-Cap	10%
Shopify	E-Commerce	Mid-Cap	10%
Charles Schwab	Financial Services	Mid-Cap	10%
DocuSign	Software	Mid-Cap	10%
Baidu	Technology	Small-Cap	five%
Shopify	E-Commerce	Small-Cap	5%
MercadoLibre	E-Commerce	Small-Cap	five%

iShares MSCI EAFE ETF   International Markets   N/A   10%

In this example, the portfolio is severa for the duration of remarkable industries, marketplace capitalizations, and geographic regions. By spreading investments at some point of the ones instructions, the portfolio targets to reduce risk and obtain extra robust lengthy-term returns.

Chapter 6: Dividend Investing

Welcome to Chapter 6 of "Transform Your Life: Living off Passive Income, Quitting Your Job, and Achieving Financial Freedom - A Practical Guide to Investing, Creating a Passive Income Stream, and Gaining Greater Economic and Personal Security in Your Life." In this financial ruin, we are able to be discussing the idea of dividend making an funding and its characteristic in building a passive income circulate.

Dividend making an funding is a famous funding technique that focuses on making an investment in stocks that pay dividends. Dividends are part of a agency's earnings which is probably paid out to shareholders on a regular foundation. Dividend making an investment is an appealing choice for those in search of to generate passive earnings because it gives a everyday flow of profits without requiring the sale of the underlying asset.

The electricity of dividends lies of their capability to compound over time. Reinvesting dividends can reason wonderful boom for your investment portfolio. This is called compounding, wherein the returns generated through the usage of your preliminary investment are reinvested to generate further returns. Over time, compounding can result in exponential growth on your investment portfolio, allowing you to benefit your economic desires faster.

Dividend making an investment is likewise an attractive preference for those seeking out balance of their investments. Companies that pay dividends have a propensity to be well-installed and financially solid. By making an funding in those agencies, traders can gain from their regular income and the following dividend payments.

In this bankruptcy, we are able to delve deeper into the arena of dividend making an funding, discussing the benefits and dangers related to this investment method. We may also even offer practical advice on a manner to get began with dividend making an funding, collectively with deciding on the right shares, dealing with your portfolio, and reinvesting your dividends for max increase. By the prevent of this chapter, you may have a strong understanding of the power of dividends and the way to leverage them to gather a a success passive earnings waft.

6.1 Types of dividend-paying shares

Dividend-paying stocks are shares that pay a element of their profits to shareholders in the shape of dividends. These shares are famous among investors who are searching for a regular skip of earnings from their investments. There are absolutely one among a type styles of dividend-paying stocks, every with their personal tendencies and advantages.

1. Blue-chip shares: Blue-chip stocks are stocks of well-installation, financially sound organizations which have an prolonged history of paying dividends. These companies

are generally leaders of their industries and feature a validated music report of fulfillment. Blue-chip shares are considered to be a number of the most secure investments within the inventory market.

2. Utility stocks: Utility shares are stocks of companies that offer crucial services together with strength, fuel, and water. These companies have a sturdy customer base and generate constant cash flows, making them appealing to traders looking for consistent dividend income.

3. Real estate funding trusts (REITs): REITs are groups that non-public and control profits-generating real assets houses such as apartment houses, workplace houses, and purchasing facilities. REITs are required to distribute at the least ninety% of their taxable profits to shareholders within the shape of dividends, making them a famous choice for buyers searching out high dividend yields.

4. Dividend aristocrats: Dividend aristocrats are groups which have extended their

dividends for as a minimum 25 consecutive years. These organizations are normally big, installed organizations with a records of sturdy financial generic performance.

five. Small-cap dividend stocks: Small-cap dividend stocks are shares of smaller businesses that pay dividends. These groups can also have less financial balance than blue-chip stocks, however they will offer better dividend yields and more capability for increase.

Investors might also moreover select to put money into one or more of those kinds of dividend-paying shares based totally on their funding dreams and chance tolerance. It is critical to conduct thorough research and evaluation earlier than making an funding in any inventory, which incorporates dividend-paying stocks. Investors have to don't forget elements which consist of the enterprise organisation's monetary fitness, dividend facts, and increase functionality earlier than making investment alternatives.

Type of Dividend-Paying Stock Characteristics

Blue-chip stocks Well-set up, financially sound businesses with an extended facts of paying dividends. Considered to be maximum of the maximum steady investments in the stock marketplace.

Utility stocks Companies that provide crucial services which include electricity, gasoline, and water. Generate steady cash flows and trap shoppers looking for ordinary dividend profits.

Real assets investment trusts (REITs) Companies that very own and manipulate income-generating actual property residences at the side of condominium homes, administrative center buildings, and purchasing facilities. Required to distribute as a minimum 90% in their taxable profits to shareholders within the shape of dividends.

Dividend aristocrats Companies that have elevated their dividends for at the least 25 consecutive years. Typically massive, established businesses with a information of robust monetary performance.

Small-cap dividend shares Stocks of smaller groups that pay dividends. May offer higher dividend yields and more functionality for increase, but may also moreover moreover have tons an awful lot less economic stability than blue-chip shares.

6.2 Evaluating and deciding on dividend shares

When evaluating and selecting dividend shares, it is essential to recall a variety of things beyond in reality the dividend yield. First, do not forget the corporation's monetary fitness and stability. Look at the business enterprise's profits, sales growth, debt-to-equity ratio, and dividend history. Companies with consistent profits and income boom, low debt-to-fairness ratios, and a statistics of robust or developing dividends are generally an extremely good bet for dividend customers.

Another trouble to endure in mind is the enterprise the employer operates in. Some industries, together with utilities, telecommunications, and customer staples, are regarded for his or her sturdy earnings and dividends. Other industries, which includes generation and healthcare, might also additionally offer better growth potential but may not be as normal in their dividend payouts.

In addition, consider the corporation's dividend payout ratio. This is the share of earnings which is probably paid out as dividends. A organization with a excessive payout ratio may be vulnerable to slicing its dividend if its earnings decline, while a business enterprise with a lower payout ratio may also have greater room to growth its dividend through the years.

Finally, don't forget the valuation of the stock. A excessive dividend yield can be appealing, however if the stock is overvalued, it may now not be an super investment. Look at the industrial organization enterprise's fee-to-profits ratio (P/E ratio) and observe it to its friends and historic averages.

By thinking about those elements, you can look at and pick out out dividend stocks which can be in all likelihood to offer a solid earnings stream and capability for growth over the long term. It's vital to keep in mind that no funding is with out danger, and diversification is vital to managing hazard in a dividend stock portfolio.

Metric   Importance   Explanation

Dividend Yield   High   This metric measures the share of a organisation's inventory rate paid out in dividends over a 12 months. A better yield suggests a higher payout to shareholders.

Dividend Growth   High   This metric measures the rate of growth in a enterprise's dividend payouts over the years. A organization with constant and great dividend increase may be an fantastic extended-time period investment.

Payout Ratio Medium This metric measures the share of a employer's profits paid out in dividends. A higher payout ratio can also additionally mean a better threat of the enterprise slicing its dividend inside the future.

Financial Health High Evaluating a enterprise's monetary fitness, which encompass its debt-to-equity ratio and coins go with the flow, can suggest its capacity to maintain dividend payments.

Industry and Market Trends Medium It's essential to bear in mind the general health and tendencies of the enterprise and marketplace in which the enterprise operates, as this can effect its potential to keep paying dividends.

Valuation Medium Assessing a company's valuation, which embody its charge-to-profits ratio and charge-to-ebook ratio, can help determine if the stock is undervalued or overrated relative to its buddies.

This desk outlines a number of the critical thing metrics to recall while evaluating and choosing dividend stocks. While dividend yield and dividend increase are essential factors to preserve in thoughts, it's also vital to evaluate the enterprise company's financial health, payout ratio, enterprise and market dispositions, and valuation to make an knowledgeable funding choice.

6.Three Creating a dividend portfolio

Creating a dividend portfolio calls for careful hobby of numerous elements, together with your investment desires, hazard tolerance, and the modern-day monetary climate. Once you have got a easy understanding of those factors, you can begin to assemble your portfolio by means of the usage of selecting excellent dividend-paying shares from numerous industries and sectors. It is likewise vital to diversify your portfolio thru making an funding in shares with unique market capitalizations, dividend yields, and growth capability.

When deciding on stocks in your dividend portfolio, you need to be aware of the organization's monetary fitness, dividend information, and payout ratio. A enterprise with a strong balance sheet, consistent profits increase, and a information of growing dividends can be an splendid addition to your portfolio. You also can search for corporations which have a low payout ratio, which means that that they preserve a sizeable component of their profits to reinvest in the commercial business employer and fund future dividend will boom.

In addition to selecting individual shares, you could also bear in thoughts investing in dividend-centered change-traded rate variety (ETFs) or mutual fee variety. These budget provide exposure to a various institution of dividend-paying shares and can be an incredible choice for buyers looking for to simplify their portfolio and decrease their risk.

When constructing your dividend portfolio, it's far crucial to have an prolonged-term mind-set and to keep away from making impulsive investment selections based totally on brief-time period market fluctuations. Instead, attention on building a well-numerous portfolio of first rate dividend-paying shares that may generate a ordinary float of passive income through the years. By doing so, you can create a reliable deliver of income and artwork within the path of attaining your monetary dreams.

To help you get commenced on constructing your dividend portfolio, the desk beneath outlines a sample portfolio that includes quite a few dividend-paying shares from unique sectors and industries.

Company Name   Ticker Symbol   Sector Dividend Yield

Johnson & Johnson   JNJ   Healthcare   2.Fifty seven%

Procter & Gamble PG Consumer Staples 2.Forty six%

PepsiCo PEP Consumer Staples 2.Eighty %

Cisco Systems CSCO Information Technology 2.Eighty 4%

IBM IBM Information Technology four.Forty five%

ExxonMobil XOM Energy 5.15%

AT&T T Communication Services 7.22%

Realty Income Corporation O Real Estate 4.Sixty 3%

AbbVie ABBV Healthcare 4.Sixty 3%

This portfolio consists of companies from numerous sectors and industries, presenting diversification and exposure to unique marketplace situations. The dividend yields variety from 2.Forty six% to 7.22%, providing a reliable supply of passive profits. Of route, this is truly an example and not a advice. It is vital to behavior your very very personal research and due diligence in advance than making any investment selections.

In conclusion, dividend making an funding is an extraordinary approach for producing passive profits. With dividend making an investment, you could earn a ordinary income circulate whilst additionally making the most of prolonged-term capital appreciation. By making an investment in agencies which have a facts of paying dividends, you could construct a reliable supply of passive earnings so as to will let you benefit financial freedom.

One of the critical trouble blessings of dividend making an investment is that it offers a regular and reliable supply of earnings. Unlike exclusive kinds of making an investment that may be issue to market volatility, dividend-paying businesses normally have a greater solid business enterprise model and are a whole lot much less likely to experience dramatic fluctuations in inventory rate. This makes dividend making an funding an awesome desire for those looking for a regular glide of passive earnings that they may rely upon.

Another advantage of dividend making an investment is the functionality for compounding returns. By reinvesting your dividends again into the identical shares, you may take gain of the energy of compounding returns, that may help increase your funding portfolio through the years. This may be mainly beneficial for people who are looking to assemble wealth over the long term and need to see their investments broaden grade by grade over time.

Finally, dividend making an investment can be a high-quality manner to diversify your investment portfolio. By making an investment in dividend-paying stocks at some stage in a range of industries and sectors, you could unfold your chance and reduce your publicity to absolutely everyone unique marketplace or company. This can assist to shield your portfolio from market downturns and offer a extra robust deliver of passive profits.

Overall, dividend making an funding is an high-quality approach for the ones trying to generate a dependable deliver of passive profits. With the ability for compounding returns, the capability to diversify your portfolio, and the steadiness of dividend-paying groups, dividend making an investment will let you acquire your monetary goals and assemble prolonged-term wealth. So in case you're searching out a reliable supply of passive income, dividend making an investment is in reality well really worth considering.

Chapter 7: Creating Passive Income Through Entrepreneurship

Welcome to financial ruin 7, wherein we are able to find out the region of entrepreneurship and its capability to create passive income streams. Many humans dream of starting their personal business employer, but the worry of failure and uncertainty can hold them again. However, entrepreneurship can provide numerous benefits past without a doubt monetary advantage.

One of the most superb benefits of entrepreneurship is the functionality to control your very private future. As an entrepreneur, you've got the liberty to create your private time desk, pick your tasks, and make your very non-public selections. This stage of autonomy can be rather remarkable and could assist you to pursue your passions and pursuits.

Another advantage is the functionality for infinite earnings. While beginning a enterprise calls for an initial investment of time, money, and resources, the ability for boom and profitability is virtually infinite. Unlike a traditional interest, in which your income is limited by using a profits or hourly revenue, entrepreneurship lets in you to scale your enterprise enterprise and growth your profits exponentially.

Entrepreneurship can also provide a revel in of reason and which means. When you're building some thing from the floor up, you are making a tangible effect at the area round you. You have the possibility to treatment troubles, create jobs, and contribute to the monetary device.

In this bankruptcy, we can speak severa strategies for growing passive profits through entrepreneurship, along side beginning a web company, growing a product, and growing a passive earnings pass through real property or rental homes. We may find out the attitude and behavior of a success marketers, and the way to conquer commonplace worrying situations that could upward thrust up whilst starting your private organization.

If you are considering entrepreneurship as a method of creating passive profits, this financial catastrophe will offer you with the statistics and device you want to get started out. So, permit's dive in and find out the arena of entrepreneurship and its potential to convert your life.

7.1 Choosing the proper enterprise model

When it includes creating passive profits via entrepreneurship, one of the most essential selections you can make is deciding on the proper business enterprise model. There are many unique sorts of industrial enterprise fashions to select out from, each with its personal advantages and disadvantages. The secret's to discover a model that aligns at the side of your abilities, interests, and monetary dreams.

One famous business organisation version is e-change. With e-trade, you could sell bodily merchandise, virtual merchandise, or a mixture of every. You can both create your non-public merchandise or deliver them from providers, and then marketplace them via your very personal internet site or famous structures like Amazon, Etsy, or Shopify. E-trade can be a wonderful opportunity when you have a knack for advertising and marketing and profits, in addition to a passion for a particular vicinity of interest or product.

Another industrial agency model is dropshipping. With dropshipping, you set up an internet preserve and promote merchandise with out in reality maintaining any stock. Instead, you determine with a provider who handles the stock and transport. When a client places an order, the dealer ships the product proper now to the purchaser. Dropshipping can be a low-threat, low-price way to get started out with e-change, however it calls for cautious research and making plans to discover reliable suppliers and merchandise as a way to sell.

Affiliate advertising is every other well-known commercial employer version. With accomplice advertising, you sell specific human beings's products or services and earn a charge for every sale you generate. You can promote products through your personal internet internet web page or social media channels, or via famous companion networks like Amazon Associates, ClickBank, or Commission Junction. Affiliate advertising and advertising can be a exceptional opportunity when you have a big audience or following in a particular place of interest.

If you have were given got a specific capacity or understanding, you can want to preserve in thoughts supplying services as a freelancer or representative. This can embody something from writing and photo layout to social media manage and internet improvement. Freelancing can be a awesome choice in case you experience jogging independently and feature a strong portfolio of exertions to show off.

Finally, you could need to recollect growing and promoting digital merchandise like guides, e-books, or software program software. Digital products can be a wonderful supply of passive earnings as quickly as they may be created, as they will be offered time and again over again with little to no ongoing attempt. However, developing a superb digital product can take effort and time in advance.

Ultimately, the right commercial enterprise enterprise version for you may depend on your skills, pastimes, and economic dreams. It's important to cautiously keep in mind your options and do your studies before making a decision. Once you have got got chosen a organization version, you can popularity on building your brand, developing your products or services, and developing your purchaser base to create a successful and sustainable passive earnings movement.

Business Model   Advantages   Disadvantages

E-alternate   Potential for excessive income; minimal in advance expenses; flexible walking hours   Competitive marketplace; ongoing advertising and marketing efforts required

Affiliate Marketing   Minimal upfront fees; no want to create or manipulate merchandise; bendy operating hours   Commission costs can be low; restricted control over merchandise promoted

Rental Property   Steady apartment profits; capability for capital appreciation; tax benefits   Property management can be time-ingesting and costly; ability for belongings damage or vacancies

Online Course   High income margins; ability to scale without problem; passive earnings capability   Time and effort required to create a excellent path; advertising may be tough

In surrender, selecting the proper organisation version is an vital step in growing passive earnings through entrepreneurship. Consider your skills, pursuits, and financial belongings while comparing the handiest-of-a-type alternatives and pick out the only that first-rate suits your goals and way of existence.

7.2 Creating a a hit on-line company

Creating a a hit on-line commercial enterprise calls for careful planning, determination, and hard artwork. The first step is to understand a worthwhile place of interest market and amplify a completely unique promoting proposition (USP) that differentiates your commercial agency from competition. Next, select out a appropriate business enterprise model based totally for your abilities, interests, and available assets. Some popular online organisation fashions encompass:

E-trade: Selling products immediately to clients thru an internet store or market.

Affiliate advertising and advertising and marketing and marketing: Promoting high-quality people's products and incomes a charge on earnings.

Dropshipping: Partnering with a provider to sell their products without retaining stock.

Information merchandise: Creating and promoting guides, ebooks, and particular virtual content material cloth.

Membership web sites: Charging a recurring fee for get right of entry to to wonderful content or offerings.

Once you've got had been given decided on a employer version, you need to create a internet website that is simple to navigate, visually attractive, and optimized for search engines like google and yahoo like google and yahoo. This consists of choosing a domain name, selecting a net website online builder or platform, and growing exceptional content material that attracts and engages your target market.

To strain website visitors in your website, you may use numerous online advertising and advertising and marketing and marketing and advertising techniques together with search engine optimization (searching for engine advertising and advertising), social media marketing and advertising and marketing and advertising, email advertising and marketing, and pay-in line with-click (PPC) marketing. It's essential to music your metrics often and modify your advertising techniques based totally totally on data-pushed insights.

Finally, to ensure the fulfillment of your on line employer, you need to prioritize customer pleasure and offer splendid customer support. This includes supplying great services or products, responding straight away to customer inquiries and proceedings, and constructing relationships at the side of your customers through customized communication and take a look at-up.

Here is a desk outlining the important detail steps concerned in developing a a achievement on line employer:

Key Steps   Description

Identify a profitable place of interest market Research your goal marketplace and competition to find a hole inside the marketplace that you can fill.

Develop a unique selling proposition (USP) Determine what makes your commercial organization unique and the manner you could use this to attract and hold customers.

Choose a suitable business enterprise model Select a employer version that aligns together together with your abilties, pursuits, and property.

Create a internet internet site Build a website that is visually attractive, easy to navigate, and optimized for search engines like google and yahoo like google and yahoo.

Create brilliant content material material Develop content fabric that engages your goal marketplace and gives cost to your customers.

Drive visitors on your net net web page Use on-line advertising strategies which includes search engine optimization, social media

7.3 Building a passive income enterprise organisation

Building a passive earnings commercial business enterprise calls for time, strive, and determination, but it may be a rewarding and worthwhile undertaking. One of the keys to fulfillment is to grow to be privy to a worthwhile area of interest that aligns together along side your skills, pastimes, and passions. This might be something from selling virtual products, to growing an internet path, to developing a cellular app. Once you've got identified your area of interest, it's important to increase a robust advertising and marketing and marketing method that includes your goals, target market, advertising and advertising techniques, and sales streams.

One effective way to generate passive income is thru companion advertising and marketing.

This entails selling distinct people's products or services and incomes a price on every sale. To be successful as an partner marketer, you want to assemble recall at the side of your target market through manner of manner of imparting precious content fabric material and sincere reviews. You moreover need to select out merchandise which is probably applicable and beneficial to your audience, and that have a high conversion fee.

Another manner to construct a passive profits commercial company is through developing and selling digital products, along side ebooks, publications, or templates. This calls for some in advance funding of time and sources to develop splendid content material fabric material, but at the same time as you've created it, you could sell it a couple of times without any extra strive. You can also use structures like Amazon or Etsy to sell physical products, which include hand-crafted crafts or print-on-call for products.

In addition to selling merchandise, you may also generate passive earnings thru advertising and marketing and marketing revenue. This involves setting advertisements in your net internet site or social media channels and making a living based absolutely totally on clicks or impressions. To maximize your advertising and advertising sales, it's important to select out commercials which might be applicable in your audience and that don't interfere with the patron enjoy.

Ultimately, building a passive earnings commercial agency calls for a combination of creativity, patience, and strategic making plans. By figuring out a profitable location of hobby, developing a strong advertising approach, and leveraging numerous profits streams, you could create a a success and sustainable supply of passive profits.

Table: Pros and Cons of Different Passive Income Business Models

Business Model   Pros   Cons

Affiliate Marketing - Low startup prices - Requires building an audience and establishing take delivery of as actual with

- No stock or shipping fees - Earnings are dependent on the achievement of the product

- Flexible and can be finished from anywhere - May require a excellent amount of time to generate ROI

Digital Products - High-earnings margins - Requires investment of time and resources to create

- Can be offered more than one instances without extra - Requires advertising and advertising to assemble cognizance and strain profits

attempt - May be situation to opposition from comparable merchandise

Advertising - Passive earnings from internet site or social media - Earnings are dependent on net site web page site site visitors and engagement

channels - Ads may be intrusive or negatively effect client enjoy

- No inventory or delivery charges - Earnings won't be big counting on website

- website on line visitors and advert placement

In conclusion, growing passive income via entrepreneurship is a effective tool for achieving financial freedom and extra non-public and financial protection. The benefits of entrepreneurship are numerous, together with the capability to manipulate your non-public future, the capability for endless profits, and the opportunity to pursue your passions and hobbies. While entrepreneurship may be tough and calls for difficult artwork and determination, the potential rewards are massive. By building a a fulfillment employer, you could generate passive earnings which can offer for you and your circle of relatives for future years.

One of the critical trouble benefits of entrepreneurship is the capability for passive earnings. Unlike conventional employment, wherein you convert it slow for a earnings, as an entrepreneur, you could construct a commercial employer that generates income even on the same time as you aren't actively running. By growing structures and strategies that allow your commercial enterprise to run without difficulty without your regular input, you may revel in a everyday flow into of profits that requires minimal effort in your element. This can provide a sizeable diploma of economic freedom, as you're not reliant on a unmarried supply of earnings and can experience extra flexibility and manage over your life.

Chapter 8: Maximizing Passive Income Through Side Hustles

Welcome to monetary wreck 8 of "Transform Your Life: Living off Passive Income, Quitting Your Job, and Achieving Financial Freedom - A Practical Guide to Investing, Creating a Passive Income Stream, and Gaining Greater Economic and Personal Security in Your Life." In this monetary disaster, we are able to communicate the importance of element hustles in maximizing your passive profits potential.

A issue hustle is a interest or commercial company that you may begin at the factor of your normal interest or number one supply of income. It is a manner to earn extra cash whilst pursuing your passions or pursuits. With the upward push of the gig monetary system, there are various opportunities for humans to start thing hustles and create passive earnings streams.

The charge of a component hustle lies in its potential to provide more earnings and diversify your house of revenue. By having multiple streams of profits, you reduce your reliance on a single supply of profits and increase your monetary safety. A facet hustle also can offer an opportunity to find out new pursuits and boom new skills, that can bring about non-public and expert increase.

Moreover, a facet hustle may be a manner to pursue your entrepreneurial desires with out leaving your entire-time interest. Many a fulfillment companies have commenced as aspect hustles, which embody well-known businesses like Airbnb and Uber.

In this financial disaster, we can discover diverse element hustle mind that you can begin to generate passive income, in addition to suggestions for coping with some time and balancing your aspect hustle at the facet of your particular commitments. By the stop of this monetary catastrophe, you will have a higher facts of the advantages of facet hustles and the manner they permit you to benefit economic freedom.

8.1 Types of issue hustles for passive earnings

If you are looking for to maximize your passive income via component hustles, there are a number of options to be had to you. One famous preference is to monetize a interest or know-how you've got already were given. For example, if you experience images, you may sell your snap shots thru inventory photos net web sites or create your very personal photography internet site and promote prints.

Another opportunity is to end up an associate marketer. This includes promoting services or products on your internet web web page or social media structures and incomes a charge for each sale made thru your specific accomplice link. Affiliate advertising and marketing and advertising and advertising and marketing is a well-known preference as it requires very little in advance funding and can be finished from everywhere within the international.

If you have got got a information for writing, you may do not forget beginning a blog or writing an eBook. By building an target market and promoting your content material fabric effectively, you can generate a regular pass of passive earnings from advertising and marketing earnings or eBook income.

Investing in real property is another famous opportunity for developing passive income. This can contain shopping for condo homes, investing in real property crowdfunding systems, or perhaps flipping houses. While real property investing can be a sizeable in advance investment, it can moreover generate full-size returns through the years.

Finally, you may don't forget investing in dividend-paying stocks or particular investments that provide passive earnings streams. This can encompass making an investment in REITs (Real Estate Investment Trusts), which permit you to invest in actual property without the hassle of property manipulate, or making an funding in dividend-paying mutual budget or alternate-traded finances (ETFs).

When deciding on a side hustle for passive income, it's far vital to recollect your strengths and hobbies, in addition to the functionality incomes capability and time dedication involved. Some side hustles may additionally additionally moreover require large in advance investment or ongoing time commitments, at the equal time as others may be greater passive and require a lot much less protection. Ultimately, the key is to find out a side hustle that works for you and permits you gain your financial goals.

Below is a table outlining a few examples of side hustles for passive earnings:

Side Hustle   Description   Potential Earnings   Time Commitment

Stock pictures   Sell your pics through inventory photos internet websites or create your very non-public pictures internet website and promote prints $50-$500+ in step with month   Low

Affiliate marketing   Promote products or services in your internet site or social media systems and earn a fee for each sale made via your particular companion link $one hundred-$10,000+ in keeping with month   Low to moderate

Blogging   Create a weblog and monetize it thru marketing profits or eBook earnings $one hundred-$10,000+ in line with month   Moderate

Rental houses   Buy rental homes and generate passive profits thru rent payments $500-$5,000+ in keeping with month   High

Real estate crowdfunding   Invest in real estate crowdfunding structures and earn passive income via dividend payments $100-$1,000+ in line with month   Low to slight

Dividend-paying shares   Invest in dividend-paying shares or other investments that provide passive earnings streams   Varies Low to slight

8.2 Building a a achievement aspect hustle

Building a successful difficulty hustle takes time, effort, and self-control. The secret is to begin small and assemble progressively, leveraging your talents and interests to create a likely deliver of passive income. Some vital factors to recall while constructing a side hustle embody selecting the right region of interest, figuring out your target marketplace, developing outstanding services or products, and advertising and marketing and advertising effectively. It's moreover crucial to be bendy and adaptable, willing to make modifications and pivot as wanted based totally totally on marketplace call for and exceptional elements.

One of the great strategies to assemble a a hit thing hustle is to recognition on providing price on your customers or clients. This technique growing products or services that resolve actual troubles or meet actual dreams inside the market. By doing so, you could differentiate yourself from opposition and bring together a committed customer base.

Another crucial trouble is to spend money on advertising and marketing and advertising and selling. This consists of leveraging social media platforms, developing content material cloth together with weblog posts and movement images, and accomplishing out to capability customers via email advertising and marketing and advertising and distinctive channels. It's important to music your consequences and make changes as had to ensure that your marketing and advertising and marketing efforts are powerful and efficient.

In addition to the ones techniques, it is also essential to have a clean plan for managing a while and sources correctly. This would possibly encompass setting goals, prioritizing duties, and delegating responsibilities as preferred. By doing so, you could avoid burnout and make sure that your side hustle remains a sustainable and interesting supply of passive profits.

Overall, building a a fulfillment facet hustle calls for staying power, staying power, and a willingness to have a look at and adapt. With the right techniques and attitude, but, everyone can flip their abilities and pursuits proper right right into a thriving supply of passive profits.

Side Hustle Idea	Time Commitment	Potential Earnings	Difficulty Level
Dog Walking/Sitting	Part-time, flexible	$two hundred-$500/month	Easy
Freelance Writing	Part-time, bendy	$500-$1,000/month	Medium
Online Teaching/Tutoring	Part-time, bendy	$500-$2,000/month	Medium
Social Media Management	Part-time, bendy	$1,000-$2,500/month	Medium
Dropshipping/E-commerce	Full-time, flexible	$5,000-$10,000+/month	Difficult

This table includes some common aspect hustle thoughts, collectively with the predicted time willpower required, capability income, and trouble degree. Of path, the ones numbers will variety relying on a desire of things, however this gives readers an idea of what to expect and may assist them decide which aspect hustle is probably the great healthy for their lifestyle and monetary goals.

eight.Three Scaling your element hustle for added profits

Once you've got got mounted a worthwhile aspect hustle, the following step is to scale it up for even more income potential. Scaling your side hustle consists of growing production, increasing your customer base, and automating techniques to reduce workload and growth general performance. One way to scale your facet hustle is to outsource obligations to freelancers or digital assistants. For example, in case you run a weblog or social media advertising and marketing and advertising and marketing business employer, you can lease freelance writers or social media managers to create content fabric and manage debts for you. This frees up some time to consciousness on better-diploma responsibilities together with strategizing and developing your organization. Another manner to scale your side hustle is to discover new markets or merchandise. If you're selling physical products, you may increase your inventory to provide extra variety to your customers. Alternatively, you can discover new markets or demographics to acquire a far broader target market. For example, if you promote home made rings on Etsy, you may undergo in thoughts growing your marketplace to embody guys's rings or personalized bridal ceremony affords. Finally, you may automate strategies to your organization to growth performance and reduce workload. This can incorporate the use of software program application to govern stock or automate advertising and marketing and marketing campaigns, or outsourcing obligations to automation machine alongside facet chatbots. By automating techniques, you can reduce the amount of time and effort required to run your thing hustle, allowing you to attention on growth and increasing profits. The following desk gives a few examples of automation equipment that can be used to streamline your issue hustle.

Tool	Function
Hootsuite	Social media manage
Trello	Project control
Asana	Task manipulate
Shopify	E-change platform
Mailchimp	Email advertising automation
Zapier	Automation device for internet apps
Canva	Graphic format and branding tool
Google Analytics	Web analytics

In give up, scaling your issue hustle is important to developing your passive profits capability. By outsourcing obligations, exploring new markets, and automating strategies, you could develop your enterprise agency and increase your revenue. The key's to live flexible and open to new opportunities, at the same time as staying actual to your specific organization model and vision.

In end, facet hustles offer a powerful manner to beautify your passive earnings glide and accelerate your journey towards economic freedom.

By leveraging your abilities, competencies, and interests, you could create multiple income streams that generate coins at the same time as you sleep.

The splendor of a aspect hustle is that it may be started with minimal investment, and it could be scaled up through the years to generate large income.

Moreover, a element hustle offers you with a diploma of pliability and manage over your profits, allowing you to earn as a whole lot or as little as you want.

By diversifying your profits streams via aspect hustles, you may additionally create a greater solid and dependable deliver of passive profits.

Rather than counting on a unmarried deliver of earnings, inclusive of a procedure or a unmarried funding, you can unfold your threat throughout multiple income streams, ensuring that you have a consistent drift of cash coming in, no matter the truth that one in each of your streams dries up.

In addition, factor hustles offer a manner to pursue your passions and hobbies at the identical time as generating income.

This can cause a extra revel in of success and satisfaction in your existence, as well as presenting an possibility to make bigger new capabilities and studies.

Chapter 9: Achieving Financial Freedom

Welcome to Chapter nine of Transform Your Life: Living off Passive Income, Quitting Your Job, and Achieving Financial Freedom - A Practical Guide to Investing, Creating a Passive Income Stream, and Gaining Greater Economic and Personal Security in Your Life. In this financial ruin, we are able to discover the final goal of passive income: attaining monetary freedom.

Financial freedom manner having sufficient passive earnings to cover all of your expenses and hold your preferred lifestyle without counting on a conventional approach. It way having the liberty to pursue your passions and pastimes, tour the area, spend time at the side of your own family, and experience the cease result of your difficult paintings.

For many humans, monetary freedom can also look like an no longer possible dream. However, with the resource of implementing the techniques we've protected in this ebook, which incorporates dividend making an investment, entrepreneurship, and factor hustles, you could assemble a reliable passive earnings circulate and paintings toward mission economic freedom.

Imagine waking up every morning with the freedom to select the way you spend some time, whether or not or now not or not it's far running on a new mission, visiting the world, or clearly exciting collectively with your own family. This is the closing cause of passive income, and it's miles feasible with the proper mind-set, strength of mind, and method.

Throughout this economic disaster, we are capable of find out realistic steps you can take to achieve economic freedom, which encompass placing clean goals, growing a plan to your passive income movement, and handling your budget correctly. By the surrender of this bankruptcy, you could have a clean understanding of what it takes to obtain economic freedom and the steps you may take to get there. So, allow's dive in!

nine.1 Calculating your monetary freedom big variety

Calculating your financial freedom huge variety is a crucial step in achieving financial independence. It is the quantity of passive profits you want to generate to cover your fees and live the lifestyles you preference with out relying on a conventional challenge. To calculate your financial freedom variety, you first need to decide your monthly fees. This includes all your bills, together with hire, utilities, groceries, transportation, and every other crucial expenses. You ought to additionally detail in any discretionary spending, together with consuming out, enjoyment, or journey.

Once you have got were given calculated your monthly fees, you want to multiply that massive range with the aid of 12 to get your annual prices. Next, you need to determine your chosen passive profits waft. This must come from plenty of assets, which encompass apartment houses, dividend-paying shares, or a business enterprise assignment. You will want to estimate the common annual charge of go again you anticipate from each funding and adjust for taxes and inflation.

Finally, you could calculate your monetary freedom range thru dividing your annual fees with the aid of using your expected annual passive income. For instance, in case your annual expenses are $50,000 and you anticipate to earn a mean annual go again of 8% in your investments, you will want a portfolio of $625,000 to generate $50,000 in annual passive profits.

It is critical to look at that your financial freedom amount isn't a one-time calculation however an ongoing technique. You want to frequently evaluation and adjust your costs, investments, and predicted returns to ensure you are at the right track to carrying out your economic dreams.

By calculating your financial freedom extensive range, you may create a roadmap to monetary independence and make informed selections approximately your investments and spending. It might also moreover take time and effort to attain your financial freedom variety, but with willpower and perseverance, you could reap the freedom and protection that consists of passive earnings.

The following table gives an example of the manner to calculate your monetary freedom range primarily based totally totally on special charges of move returned and annual costs:

Annual Expenses   three% Rate of Return   5% Rate of Return   7% Rate of Return

$30,000 $one million $six hundred,000 $428,571

$50,000 $1,666,667 $one million $714,286

$75,000 $2,500,000 $1,500,000 $1,071,429

$100,000 $three,333,333 $2,000,000 $1,428,571

As you could see, the higher your annual costs, the more money you may want to accumulate if you want to accumulate monetary freedom. Additionally, the better your charge of pass decrease returned, the less cash you will want to build up at the way to generate the same quantity of passive income. It is crucial to keep in thoughts each of these factors even as determining your economic freedom range.

nine.2 Strategies for achieving economic freedom

Once you have got got calculated your economic freedom range, the subsequent step is to place into impact strategies to help you benefit that goal. Here are a few strategies you may use to acquire financial freedom:

1. Reduce Your Expenses: The masses a lot much less you spend, the greater you may hold and invest. To lessen your prices, create a budget and track your spending. Look for techniques to lessen on useless charges like

dining out or shopping for things you do no longer need. Consider downsizing your house or car to shop coins on housing and transportation prices.

2. Increase Your Income: Increasing your income will assist you to obtain your economic freedom variety faster. You can try this via inquiring for a decorate at paintings, beginning a detail hustle or freelance paintings, making an funding in stocks or real property, or growing a passive profits bypass.

three. Save and Invest: Saving and making an investment your cash is vital for conducting financial freedom. Set up automated monetary savings and funding contributions every month. Invest in a special portfolio of shares, bonds, and actual belongings to maximise your returns and decrease your risks.

four. Pay off Debt: High-hobby debt may be a high impediment to reaching financial freedom. Make a plan to pay off your debt as quickly as viable. Consider consolidating your debt or negotiating with lenders to decrease your interest expenses.

five. Stay Focused and Committed: Achieving financial freedom takes time, challenge, and staying strength. Stay targeted on your goals and decide to creating clever financial choices each day. Celebrate your successes along the way and observe out of your errors.

Here is a table summarizing the vital element techniques for reaching economic freedom:

Strategy	Description
Reduce Your Expenses	Cut back on needless spending to shop extra money every month.
Increase Your Income	Find techniques to boom your income through artwork, side hustles, making an funding, or passive profits streams.
Save and Invest	Save and make investments your cash in a numerous portfolio of shares, bonds, and real estate.

Pay off Debt   Make a plan to repay immoderate-interest debt as quickly as feasible.

Stay Focused and Committed   Stay focused to your dreams and commit to making smart monetary picks every day.

By imposing those strategies, you can achieve financial freedom and experience the peace of thoughts and safety that consists of it.

9.Three Overcoming barriers and staying endorsed

While the adventure to accomplishing economic freedom is profitable, it isn't always continuously clean. You will possibly face obstacles along the manner that could derail your improvement or reason you to lose motivation. The secret is to live focused for your purpose and find tactics to conquer those limitations. One commonplace obstacle is the temptation to invest in topics that are not important or do now not align collectively with your desires. It may be tempting to splurge on a luxury object or take an pricey tour, but those alternatives can set you decrease lower back notably for your course to financial freedom. Another obstacle is the concern of failure. Starting a cutting-edge commercial company or making an investment within the stock market can be intimidating, and the possibility of failure can be discouraging. To conquer this, it is important to remember that failure is a herbal part of the getting to know technique and might offer treasured training for future success. You also can are trying to find out resource from others who've been via similar reports, along with a mentor or a network of like-minded humans. Finally, it's far essential to live advocated and centered for your goals. Celebrate your successes, no matter how small, and keep music of your development to remind yourself of strategies a long way you have got come. Find methods to live inspired, such as studying success memories or working towards gratitude for what you have got completed to this point. With dedication, perseverance, and a notable mind-set, you could triumph over barriers and acquire the economic freedom you desire.

To help you stay stimulated and focused, you could use a table to tune your improvement and display your financial dreams. Here is an instance desk:

Goal	Start Date	End Date	Amount Needed	Amount Saved	Progress
Emergency Fund	January 1, 2023	December 31, 2023	$10,000	$6,000	60%
Pay Off Credit Card Debt	January 1, 2023	December 31, 2023	$five,000	$2,000	40%
Invest in Stock Market	January 1, 2024	December 31, 2024	$10,000	$zero	zero%
Purchase Rental Property	January 1, 2026	December 31, 2026	$50,000	$0	0%

This desk permits you to visualise your improvement inside the path of your economic goals and make changes as favored. By monitoring your progress, you can see how some distance you have come and live added directly to hold going. It additionally can help you grow to be aware of regions in which you may need to regulate your approach or increase your monetary savings to stay on path. Overall, thru the use of using strategies to overcome obstacles and tracking your development, you could accumulate monetary freedom and create the life you desire.

In stop, undertaking economic freedom via passive profits isn't always just a dream, however a sensible intention that can be performed with determination, place, and staying power. By building a numerous portfolio of investments, developing a passive income movement thru dividend making an investment, entrepreneurship, and aspect hustles, you may create a robust deliver of income that requires minimal attempt to maintain.

The closing cause of passive profits is to loose yourself from the regulations of traditional employment, supplying you with the liberty to pursue your passions and live the existence you choice. Whether it's miles touring the area, beginning a organization, or genuinely spending greater time along with your own family, passive profits can provide the manner to attain your goals.

By following the sensible recommendations and strategies cited on this guide, you may take control of your financial destiny and reap the monetary freedom you deserve.

Remember that building a passive income flow takes effort and time, however the rewards are well certainly worth it. With patience and perseverance, you can redecorate your life, stay off passive earnings, stop your activity, and gather economic freedom.

Chapter 10: Living Your Best Life

Welcome to Chapter 10 of "Transform Your Life: Living off Passive Income, Quitting Your Job, and Achieving Financial Freedom." In this financial disaster, we are able to discover how passive income assist you to stay your first-class lifestyles.

Living your amazing existence technique severa matters to high-quality human beings. For some, it would mean having the liberty to adventure the world or pursue a hobby they're enthusiastic about. For others, it is able to be the capacity to spend extra time with family or sincerely live a strain-unfastened existence. Whatever your definition may be, the commonplace denominator for undertaking it's miles financial freedom.

Financial freedom way having enough passive earnings to cowl your expenses and residing a lifestyles loose from the regulations of conventional employment. Passive income lets in you to earn cash at the same time as you sleep, releasing up a while to pursue what topics maximum to you. With passive earnings, you can pick out wherein you need to live, what you need to do, and the way you need to spend it gradual.

Passive profits is the crucial difficulty to residing your fantastic existence as it affords the closing freedom and flexibility to live lifestyles to your private phrases. It permits you to pursue your passions, spend time with cherished ones, and live a life with out economic worry. And the awesome element is that passive income is workable for everyone who's inclined to region in the effort and time to create it.

In this bankruptcy, we're able to discover severa methods to maximize your passive profits streams and hints at the way to reap economic freedom. We will even discuss the manner to create a existence that aligns together collectively with your values and passions, permitting you to simply stay your excellent lifestyles. So, permit's dive in and find out how passive earnings allow you to gain your goals and stay your great lifestyles.

10.1 Living the lifestyles you need with passive income

Living the existence you want with passive income is the closing cause of accomplishing economic freedom. When you have were given were given sufficient passive income to cover your residing expenses, you've got were given the liberty to live life in your very own terms. You can select out to adventure the arena, spend greater time at the side of your circle of relatives, pursue your passions, or without a doubt experience your loose time with out the priority of a traditional interest. Passive earnings gives you with the capacity to make alternatives that align together along with your values and priorities.

One instance of that is the tale of John, who worked in business enterprise America for over a long time in advance than determining to pursue his ardour for pics. With the help of his passive earnings streams, John come to be able to leave his challenge and start his very non-public snap shots organization, which he now runs whole-time. He now not has to worry approximately the every day grind of a 9-to-five assignment and has the freedom to pursue his ardour and tour the arena.

Another example is Sarah, who used her passive profits to create a greater bendy lifestyle that allowed her to spend greater time in conjunction with her youngsters. With her condo homes producing normal income, Sarah have become capable of lessen her jogging hours and take greater day without work to be together together with her own family. She no longer has to choose out amongst spending time along with her youngsters and earning a residing.

These examples illustrate how passive earnings can offer you with the economic protection and freedom to pursue the lifestyles you genuinely need. However, it is crucial to word that carrying out economic freedom and building passive income streams takes time, attempt, and situation. It requires steady saving, making an investment, and clever preference-making. But with determination and a easy plan, you can create a existence that aligns collectively together with your values and priorities.

Ultimately, the intention of passive profits is not pretty an awful lot conducting financial freedom, however additionally approximately growing a existence that brings you happiness and achievement. It is ready having the functionality to make alternatives that align at the side of your dreams and values, and dwelling a lifestyles that you are in fact obsessed with.

10.2 Finding fulfillment beyond monetary freedom

Living the life you want with passive profits is an extraordinary feeling this is inner attain for anyone inclined to vicinity within the effort to create a everyday pass of earnings that doesn't require lively artwork. With passive income, you've got were given were given the capability to live a extra fulfilled lifestyles with the resource of getting the time and belongings to attention at the subjects that virtually consider to you. Here are a few sensible examples of techniques you could use your passive income to convert your existence:

Examples   How it permit you to collect your goals

Traveling the arena   With passive income, you may excursion to your dream locations with out disturbing approximately the rate or the day without work art work. Imagine spending some months in Europe, visiting ancient landmarks, attempting new substances, and experiencing superb cultures. With passive income, you may make it a truth.

Starting a business company   Do you've got a ardour for entrepreneurship but do no longer have the charge variety or the time to start a commercial business enterprise? Passive earnings can offer you with the capital and the liberty to pursue your desires. You can use your passive earnings to invest in a commercial corporation, hire personnel, and assemble your logo with out sacrificing your non-public lifestyles.

Pursuing a interest   If you have got have been given a hobby that you're passionate about but in no way have enough time to commit to it, passive earnings can help. With a steady waft of profits coming in, you may spend more time pursuing your interests, whether or now not or now not it's far portray, playing song, or trekking.

Investing in real property   Real belongings is a tested manner to generate passive income, and it could be an extremely good manner to reap financial freedom. With passive earnings from apartment houses, you could cowl your dwelling charges and assemble wealth through the years.

These are only a few examples of the manner passive earnings let you obtain your dreams and live the lifestyles you need. However, growing passive earnings streams isn't always a get-rich-short scheme. It takes time, try, and backbone to bring together a a hit passive profits portfolio. Here are a few realistic recommendations to help you get started out out:

1. Define your goals: Before you begin growing passive income streams, you need to have a clear idea of what you want to obtain. Do you want to retire early, excursion the place, or begin a commercial agency? Once you recognize your dreams, you can create a plan to accumulate them.

2. Choose the right passive earnings streams: There are many strategies to generate passive income, inclusive of making an investment in shares, rental properties, and growing virtual products. Choose the streams that align together collectively along with your goals and which you experience doing.

3. Invest for your schooling: To acquire fulfillment in growing passive income, you need to invest in your education. Read books,

take publications, and take a look at from professionals within the area. The more you recognise, the higher you could make informed selections and collect a worthwhile portfolio.

four. Be affected man or woman and continual: Building passive earnings takes time and effort. It's critical to stay dedicated on your desires and be continual on your efforts. Even in case you face setbacks, preserve going, and observe from your mistakes.

In surrender, living the life you need with passive profits is possible. With the right thoughts-set, dreams, and strategies, you can assemble a regular motion of income that permits you to recognition on the matters that be counted to you. So start these days, put money into your destiny, and revel in the liberty and safety that passive earnings can offer.

10.Three Giving decrease returned and creating a distinction

While economic freedom is an essential component of residing your top notch life, it isn't the handiest problem that contributes on your easy achievement. Finding fulfillment beyond economic freedom is crucial to living a honestly satisfied and exciting existence. Here are a few realistic examples of methods you can discover fulfillment past economic freedom:

1. Pursue your passions: One of the great strategies to discover success past economic freedom is to pursue your passions. Whether it is writing, painting, or playing music, doing something you like can supply a feel of purpose and delight to your existence. Don't be afraid to attempt new matters and discover taken into consideration one in all a type hobbies till you find what really resonates with you.

2. Give lower returned for your community: Volunteering a while and skills to assist others is every other way to find out success past monetary freedom. Whether it is through a

neighborhood charity or a international corporation, giving decrease returned can offer a revel in of cause and pleasure that cash can not purchase.

3. Focus in your relationships: Building and preserving full-size relationships together with your circle of relatives is essential to finding achievement past economic freedom. Take the time to connect to your circle of relatives and pals, and prioritize the folks that depend maximum to you.

four. Travel and enjoy new cultures: Traveling and experiencing new cultures is any other manner to find out success beyond monetary freedom. Exploring new locations, meeting new humans, and trying new additives can boom your horizons and provide a feel of adventure and excitement.

Chapter 11: Types Of Passive Income

Before going over the unique varieties of passive earnings, it is vital to have a look at that they may be a remarkable way to help you generate extra money go with the flow, whether or no longer or now not you are on foot a factor commercial corporation or absolutely looking to get a piece more money each month, especially as inflation rages at some point of the financial system.

With passive earnings, you could have coins coming in on the equal time as you figure your primary employment, or in case you're capable to accumulate a strong go with the waft of passive profits, you may want to take a hint day without work.

The concept of getting coins through passive income may additionally moreover enchantment to you if you're worried about being able to maintain sufficient of your income to attain your retirement goals.

Passive income: What is it?

The Internal Revenue Service (IRS) states that passive earnings consists of everyday profits from a deliver apart from an business enterprise or contractor and can come from considered one in every of topics: condominium property or a corporation in which one isn't actively involved, which incorporates receiving e-book royalties or stock dividends.

In truth, you could perform a little or all the art work up the front, but retaining passive profits generally requires a few more art work through the years, which includes retaining your product up to date or your condominium property properly-maintained.

But if you stay with the plan, it may be a superb way to make cash and you'll advantage a few extra financial safety alongside the way.

It's no longer passive sales.

Your art work: Typically, passive income does not come from a supply in which you have had a massive hobby, including the pay you acquire from a pastime.

Getting a second mission: Passive income is prepared putting in a steady movement of income without you having to install a whole lot of paintings to get it, so getting a 2d pastime is not going to qualify as a passive earnings glide.

Non-dividend-paying shares or assets like cryptocurrencies can be thrilling, however they might not produce passive income for you. Investing may be a top notch manner to create passive profits, but satisfactory if the belongings you very very own pay dividends or hobby.

The hints for constructing wealth with passive income are listed below.

Rental Earnings

The cash earned from renting out belongings, together with a residence, rental, or commercial enterprise place, is known as condominium earnings. Rental income is a notable manner to generate a regular motion of coins waft at the identical time as no longer having to sell the belongings or do an entire lot ongoing paintings.

Renting out real belongings is a awesome approach to generate passive income, but it often takes extra paintings than people count on.

You risk losing your funding in case you do not make an effort to learn how to make it beneficial.

Possibility: According to Graves, with a purpose to generate passive sales from condo houses, you want to decide on three factors:

Your favored rate of income on funding

The average charges and charges for the assets

The charges related to owning the belongings

You could want to fee $three,133 in monthly lease to acquire your intention, as an example, in case your aim is to earn $10,000 a

12 months in condo coins go with the flow and the assets has a $2,000 month-to-month mortgage and a further $three hundred a month in taxes and one of a kind prices.

Risk: There are a few matters to bear in mind, like whether or now not there may be a marketplace for your property, what could probably take place if you hire to a renter who would now not pay on time or damages the belongings, and what also can take vicinity when you have hassle renting out your property. Any of these things may want to noticeably reduce your passive profits.

You'll need to weigh the ones risks and function contingency plans in area. You also can unexpectedly have tenants who cannot pay their rent, on the identical time as you could no matter the reality that have a loan of your private to pay; you could now not be able to hire the house out for as plenty as you could before; and home charges have been developing rapid due in thing to pretty low loan charges, so your rents won't be able to cowl your fees.

Rental Property Types

You ought to have interaction in an entire lot of condo homes, along with:

Single-circle of relatives houses, metropolis-houses, and houses which can be leased to humans on their very very own or as part of a circle of relatives are examples of residential rental houses.

Office houses, retail institutions, and warehouses are examples of business apartment houses which may be leased to agencies.

Vacation condo homes - These are houses which is probably leased out for short remains, like the ones listed on VRBO or Airbnb.

Selecting a Rental Home

There are quite a few of things to bear in mind at the equal time as selecting a condo assets:

Location: Look for houses in properly-favored neighborhoods in which condominium call for is strong.

Price - Check to appearance that the assets within reason priced and gives a decent pass returned on funding.

Make positive the belongings is in exquisite situation and can now not need any fundamental renovations or upkeep.

Rental call for - Take into consideration emptiness expenses and location rental name for.

Taking Care of Rental Properties

Once you have were given determined on a apartment belongings, it's far essential to cope with it efficaciously. Here are a few pointers:

Make effective to thoroughly vet ability tenants via walking credit score score rating and man or woman tests to ensure you're renting to dependable humans.

Define the condo situations honestly, which includes the month-to-month fee quantity, due date, and period of the lease.

Keep the belongings in super shape and address any preservation problems proper away.

Rent need to be paid on time, and you need to have a method in location for the way to address past due bills.

Have a manner in area to cope with vacancies, which includes advertising the apartment belongings and supplying incentives to trap new renters.

Overall, if you put money into the right property and control it properly, rental income may be a tremendous deliver of passive earnings. By using the recommendation in this text, you may gather a reliable float of condominium income that allows you to offer cash glide for years yet to come.

Dividend Income

Dividend income is a common type of passive income because it gives a constant go with the flow of coins waft with out requiring ongoing try. Dividend profits is the cash earned from keeping stocks or shares in a industrial business enterprise that distributes part of its earnings to shareholders.

Companies pay coins dividends on a quarterly basis out in their earnings, and all you need to do is personal the stock. Dividends are paid per proportion of stock, so the extra shares you private, the higher your payout. Shareholders in agencies with dividend-yielding shares collect a price from the organisation on a everyday foundation.

Opportunity: Owning dividend-paying shares may be one of the most passive methods to make cash due to the reality the income comes without delay into your brokerage account and is unrelated to any activity aside from the unique financial funding.

Risk: Choosing the best stocks is hard.

Graves cautions that too many novices enter the marketplace without very well learning the commercial enterprise enterprise issuing the inventory. "You've had been given to research every company's internet website and be comfortable with their economic statements," Graves says. "You ought to spend to 3 weeks investigating every corporation."

Graves shows the use of trade-traded finances, or ETFs, which might be investment finances that maintain shares, commodities, and bonds however trade like shares and diversify your holdings absolutely so if one commercial enterprise business enterprise cuts its payout, it does no longer have an effect on the ETF's price or dividend too much. Despite this, there are techniques to spend money on dividend-yielding stocks with out spending a sizable amount of time comparing corporations.

ETFs are a extraordinary preference for novices because of the fact they're smooth to recognize, enormously liquid, low cost, and characteristic substantially higher capability returns because of appreciably decrease costs than mutual budget, in keeping with Graves.

Another amazing chance is that stocks and ETFs can drop substantially in a quick time frame, specially in uncertain times, like in 2020 whilst the coronavirus disaster rocked the economic markets, at the equal time as numerous price range may be an entire lot much less affected by economic strain.

Dividend inventory sorts

The primary commands of dividend securities are:

Common shares are listed on a stock trade and characteristic the potential to increase in rate as well as generate dividend earnings.

Preferred stocks are securities that pay a fixed dividend fee and are paid dividends and liquidation proceeds in advance than common stocks.

Selection of Dividend Stocks

There are severa subjects to think about while selecting dividend securities, together with:

The amount of the inventory's rate that is allocated as rewards every yr is called the dividend yield.

History of dividend bills: Look for shares that have a track report of continuously developing their dividend payments through the years.

Financial balance - Assess the organisation's financial balance and functionality for future improvement.

Market conditions - Take beneath interest the general market situations and monetary outlook.

Take Care of Dividend Stocks

It's critical to correctly control your dividend shares after you've got decided on them. Here are some hints:

To spread out your risk, diversify your portfolio via making investments in some of dividend-paying agencies.

Reinvest dividends: Take into consideration reinvesting your dividends to buy extra fairness.

Track the fulfillment of your portfolio and make vital modifications with the useful resource of tracking it.

Keep knowledgeable – Keep abreast of any changes in marketplace situations that could affect the stock's price, in addition to the organisation's economic achievement.

If you invest inside the proper agencies and control your portfolio nicely, dividend income may be a wonderful supply of passive profits. By the use of the recommendation supplied proper here, you may assemble a dividend income pass so you can keep to supply coins go together with the flow for decades to return back again.

Interest Income

Interest income is a dependable shape of passive earnings which could provide a regular move of coins flow. Interest income is the cash crafted from making an funding in interest-bearing property, consisting of economic savings debts, certificates of deposit (CDs), bonds, and one-of-a-kind constant-profits devices.

Opportunities: Stable deliver of income: For those who are retired or seeking to decorate their modern-day earnings, hobby earnings can offer a robust and predictable deliver of income.

Diversification: To assist decrease threat and probable growth returns, hobby-bearing assets can be protected in a diverse monetary portfolio.

Savings payments and special steady-earnings investments, collectively with bonds, may be a reliable manner to hold money whilst earning interest.

Tax blessings: Some hobby income can also get keep of favorable tax remedy, together with federal earnings tax exemption for municipal bond interest.

Accessibility: Since banks, brokerage corporations, and distinct monetary businesses make it clean to get right of get admission to to interest-bearing investments, many customers discover them to be a to be had opportunity.

Flexibility: Interest-bearing investments give traders freedom in phrases of the manner lots cash they placed up, how lengthy they preserve it, and what type of hazard they are willing to accept.

Risk: Interest price hazard: Interest rate danger is the threat of loss due to changes in hobby costs; if prices upward push, the price of consistent-charge investments can also moreover decline and the hobby earned on variable-price investments may also furthermore decline; conversely, if fees fall, the charge of constant-rate investments may also increase however the interest earned on variable-fee investments may also moreover furthermore fall.

Credit chance is the opportunity that a borrower will now not pay off the debt, that may result in the lender losing both the crucial and any accrued interest.

Risk of loss because of a decline within the purchasing energy of cash through the years is referred to as inflation risk. If the hobby charge on an funding is much much less than the fee of inflation, the actual fee of the funding might also additionally fall.

Risk of now not being able to promote an funding rapid sufficient or at a honest rate is known as liquidity chance. If an investment is illiquid, the investor may not be capable of promote it once they want to or they'll should promote it for an awful lot much less than they paid for it.

Risk of now not being capable of reinvest the proceeds of an funding on the equal rate of pass lower back is called reinvestment chance. If hobby prices fall, an investor may not be capable of reinvest their cash at the equal rate of move returned, that may decrease their overall pass back on funding.

When making an funding in hobby-bearing property, it's miles essential to take those risks below interest and diversify your portfolio to deal with them.

Different Interest-Giving Assets

You may have interplay in a number of hobby-bearing assets, collectively with:

Savings payments are sorts of deposit money owed that credit score rating unions and banks offer that pay hobby on the money located.

Certificates of deposit (CDs) are time-primarily based monetary organization payments with higher hobby fees than financial monetary financial savings bills, however they call for a willpower over a difficult and speedy time body.

Bonds are debt devices that pay hobby to bondholders and are issued via governments or corporations.

Selecting Assets That Pay Interest

There are many things to bear in mind at the same time as choosing interest-bearing investments, at the side of:

Interest fees - Seek out investments that deliver a strong go once more on funding and characteristic aggressive hobby fees.

Consider the investment's time period because of the fact longer-term investments regularly deliver higher hobby charges.

Risk: Consider the funding's degree of hazard in advance than making the purchase. While higher-risk investments may additionally moreover provide better hobby prices, further they create a larger chance of monetary loss.

Managing Assets Bearing Interest

It's vital to cope with interest-bearing belongings efficiently as quickly as you've got determined on them. Here are some tips:

To spread out your chance, diversify your portfolio by means of using making investments in some of hobby-bearing securities.

Reinvest hobby to increase profits. Think approximately reinvesting your interest profits.

Track the fulfillment of your portfolio and make critical adjustments with the aid of monitoring it.

Keep up with marketplace traits and hobby price modifications that could affect your investments with the aid of staying educated.

Overall, in case you invest in the ideal belongings and manipulate your portfolio well, hobby profits may be a exceptional source of passive earnings. By the usage of the advice furnished proper right here, you could set up an extended-term motion of hobby profits as a way to offer coins glide..

Capital Gains

If you put money into belongings that grow in price through the years, such as shares, real assets, or one-of-a-type securities, capital profits can be a source of passive earnings. Capital income are the rise in price of an investment asset, which incorporates stocks, real belongings, or different securities.

Capital gains deliver customers the risk to in all likelihood earn higher returns than they may with distinct investment sorts, which consist of constant-earnings investments, which give lower returns but decrease risk.

Portfolio growth: As earnings from promoting property at a better rate can be reinvested in one-of-a-kind belongings or used to growth the amount of the portfolio, capital income can assist an investor's portfolio enlarge through the years.

Tax advantages: Capital profits may be hassle to favorable tax remedy depending on the investor's profits stage and the quantity of time the asset changed into saved; extended-term capital income, as an example, are taxed at a lower rate than brief-term income.

Capital earnings may be crafted from lots of asset schooling, consisting of stocks, mutual rate range, actual belongings, and distinct investments. As a forestall give up end result, they'll be a useful tool for diversifying an investor's portfolio.

Strategic making plans: By cautiously studying marketplace conditions and having an in depth knowledge of the precise asset beauty being invested in, it is easy to make capital gains through the usage of the usage of strategically purchasing assets at a discount and selling them at a top elegance.

Risks: Market danger: If the marketplace suffers a downturn, the price of an asset can decline, ensuing in a loss at the capital benefit; other dangers: Credit danger: The charge of an asset can upward thrust or fall because of changes in credit situations; political unrest; or economic downturns.

Risk associated with timing transactions: When it entails capital gains, timing is crucial. If an investor sells an asset too speedy, they hazard lacking out on functionality gains, on the identical time as within the event that they maintain onto it for too lengthy, the asset's value may additionally fall and that they threat losing out at the capital advantage.

Tax chance: Because capital gains are taxable, the tax rate may additionally furthermore variety primarily based at the investor's earnings and the protecting duration of the asset, and because of the fact tax prison suggestions and expenses can also alternate, the tax crook obligation on capital profits may additionally furthermore change.

Liquidity threat: It can be difficult to sell assets rapid, specially in the route of marketplace downturns, and if an investor should do so, they might be forced to truely accept a decrease rate than the specific purchase price, which can suggest dropping out at the capital gain.

Concentration risk: If an investor holds a huge factor in their portfolio in a single asset, they may be assignment to the risks related to that asset. For instance, if an investor holds a substantial role in a single stock, they may be vulnerable to drops inside the stock charge, which also can result in a loss on the capital gain.

Capital Gains Asset Types

A fashion of commodities can bring about capital profits, which includes:

Stocks - Investing in shares which can be brazenly traded may additionally additionally result in capital gains if the stock's really worth rises through the years.

Real estate - If the fee of your real property rises over the years, you may be able to make capital profits.

Mutual Funds: As the value of a mutual fund rises, making an investment in one which holds shares or distinctive assets also can moreover bring about capital earnings.

Profiting from Capital Gains

Selling the asset at a extra rate than the acquisition charge, whether or not right away, via the sale of stocks of a mutual fund, or via the sale of options contracts, is needed to recognize capital income.

Taking Care of Capital Gains

It's critical to efficaciously manage capital earnings as quickly as you have got invested in property that produce them. Here are a few tips:

In order to perceive chances for capital profits, hold an eye fixed on economic signs and marketplace trends.

To spread out your risk, diversify your portfolio through technique of creating an investment in pretty quite a few commodities.

Think approximately taxes - Make plans in slight of the financial ramifications of capital profits.

Keep informed – Keep abreast of changes to the marketplace environment and the success of your investments.

Overall, if you put money into the right assets and control your portfolio nicely, capital income may be a exquisite supply of passive profits. By using the recommendation provided right here, you can assemble a motion of capital income that allows you to maintain to offer coins flow for years to come.

Royalties

If you very very personal revolutionary works or highbrow belongings that produces earnings, royalties may be a supply of passive earnings. Royalties are payments made to the owner of a progressive art work or intellectual assets for the use or sale of that art work.

Different Royalties

Depending on the form of progressive artwork or intellectual property you private, there are numerous kinds of royalties you may acquire:

Music - Compositions, recordings, and stay suggests of tune can all bring about royalties.

Book purchases and translations are eligible for royalties.

Patents - When patented improvements or techniques are furnished or certified, royalties can be made.

Trademarks - When logos or business employer corporation names are certified, royalties can be earned.

Royalties are earned

Owning the rights to a creative art work or highbrow property is a prerequisite for being capable of make royalties; you could try this thru developing the paintings your self or thru shopping for the rights straight away from the author. Once you've got the rights, you may make royalties via some of channels, inclusive of licensing agreements, income, or streaming services.

Royalties, which is probably payments made to the owner of a patent, copyright, or special shape of intellectual belongings in move once more for the proper to use or sell that property, can present traders with some of possibilities, collectively with:

Opportunities: Because royalties do not require energetic manipulate of the intellectual belongings, they're a deliver of passive sales for traders.

Diversification: A form of highbrow assets classes, which consist of patents, copyrights, and emblems, can yield royalties, giving shoppers a manner to diversify their investment holdings.

High capability returns: In precise for patents and particular intellectual assets with immoderate monetary value, royalties could have a immoderate capability skip lower back.

Reduced chance: Because royalties do not require massive economic investments and the chance is shared amongst some of licensees or users, they may be lots less unstable than distinct varieties of investments.

Long-time period profits motion: Because royalties are usually paid out over a number of years, they could provide buyers an prolonged-time period profits motion.

International publicity: Because highbrow belongings rights can be licensed and offered in marketplaces everywhere inside the international, royalties can deliver traders global publicity.

However, it is essential to recognize the criminal and regulatory necessities related to proudly owning and licensing highbrow assets, similarly to the capacity risks, which encompass the possibility of infringement or adjustments in market demand for the certified product or technology. Earning royalties can normally provide investors with a completely unique opportunity to earn passive income, diversify their portfolios, and probable earn immoderate returns whilst coping with hazard effectively.

While receiving royalties can offer consumers a number of opportunities, there are risks related to it as well. These dangers embody:

Legal hazard: Investors might also moreover come across criminal stressful conditions from competition maintaining comparable highbrow assets rights, and patent and copyright infringement claims may be difficult to execute because of the complexity and jurisdictional model of intellectual belongings legal guidelines.

Market risk: If name for for a product or technology declines, the royalty payments may additionally moreover decrease or prevent absolutely.

Concentration danger: If a single licensee or user stops paying royalties or proclaims financial break, the investor's income motion can be notably suffering from the dearth of that licensee or person's royalty profits.

Technological risk: Emerging era have the functionality to render vintage contemporary-day patents and copyrights, lowering their charge and in all likelihood eliminating the income flow from royalties.

Investors may additionally run the risk of violating someone else's intellectual property rights, which can bring about jail motion and hefty financial obligations.

www.ingramcontent.com/pod-product-compliance
Lightning Source LLC
Chambersburg PA
CBHW071445080526
44587CB00014B/1999